RICHARD E. SHERRELL

THE HUMAN IMAGE:
AVANT-GARDE AND CHRISTIAN

JOHN KNOX PRESS
Richmond, Virginia

To Virginia

<hr>

Standard Book Number: 8042-1965-6
Library of Congress Catalog Card Number: 75-80274
© M. E. Bratcher 1969
Printed in the United States of America

CONTENTS

PREFACE

Whenever a member of the theological community takes it upon himself to speak with both passionate intensity and reasoned judgment (if these efforts can be achieved simultaneously) concerning the importance of the arts for theology, he immediately finds himself in a defensive position in relation both to his colleagues and to the artists he would engage in meaningful discussion. Written deep within the Christian tradition is a suspicion of the artist and his work. So long as the artist could be held in a position of craft-servitude to the dogmatic interests of the church, there was little problem. To be sure, the wealth of artistic legacy of the Greco-Roman world was a constant source of temptation to the autonomous[1] claims of the human spirit. For reasons of defense against such temptation and for more worthy apologetic reasons, the early church fathers drew upon the allegorical method of interpretation already deeply embedded in classical culture. With this method pagan art and philosophy could be turned to the uses and interests of the church. The continuation of the allegorizing method into the sixteenth and seventeenth centuries testifies to a persistent sense of uneasiness with the potent energies of a human spirit longing for autonomous expression of its own creativity. This same tension is still with us. As Gerardus van der Leeuw says in his book, *Sacred and Profane Beauty,*

Thus rivalry reigns: first, in general, rivalry between the religious spirit and the aesthetically, ethically, or scientifically oriented man; second, a much sharper and more implacable rivalry between the Christian religion and these manifestations of the intellectual world. Religion is always imperialistic. No matter how vague or general it may be, it always demands everything for itself. It can tolerate, at most, the claims made by art, ethics, and science, but it can never recognize their independent justification.[2]

The other pole of the tension is constituted by the claims for genuine autonomy made by the arts. As van der Leeuw also notes, "On the other hand, science, art, and ethics are also imperialistic, each in its own right and also in combination with the others. Each claims all of life."[3] This is especially true in our own time when culture has been fragmented into specializations. Indeed it is only in such a cultural situation that the artist is isolated and identified as such, thus experiencing within himself a certain freedom from the external restraints of an older ecclesiastical domination and perhaps a sense of loss of community within the culture at the same time. He may also, of course (and here is a note of tragedy in our time), fall prey to political domination for propaganda purposes. But more to the point, the artist is suspicious of the church and its theological pretensions as constant threats to his autonomy. The issue is intensified whenever the tradition of the artist-as-high-priest-of-the-imagination is invoked to substantiate the sacred and revelatory nature of art and of the artist's calling. We need not adduce the testimony of the ages here. Suffice it to note that poets as divergent in their sensibilities as Shelley and Joyce testify to the priestly functions of the artist.

In the more recent critical literature the question of autonomous art is asked and answered affirmatively in relation to the pressures of positivistic linguistic analysis, particularly upon poetry and its truth claims. What the critics are claiming for poetry can equally be argued for the other arts and certainly for the theatre which is the central concern here. In response to such a statement as Arthur Mizener's that poetry is only "amiable insanity,"[4] or that of I. A. Richards in his early writings on philosophy and poetry that poetry is constituted of "pseudo-statements,"[5] Allen Tate has rejoined with the assertion that "the high forms of literature offer us the only complete . . . versions of our experience."[6] While Tate's affirmation may be somewhat overly contentious, it nevertheless indicates the feeling-tone of artists when they sense that their position is threatened with outside interpretations.

With full sensibility of this stance the theological critic must undertake his task. Conversation can proceed only if both theologian and artist do somewhat more than announce an imperialistic strategy buttressed by dogmatic assertions. In what follows, an attempt will be made from the theological side to do more than tolerate the concerns and deliverances of the artist.

The study which I undertake is a theological critique of the images of man to be found in the avant-garde French theatre. Such a statement immediately calls for an indication of the limits I propose for this study.

To pursue a theological study, it is important to locate the study both within the theological tradition and with respect to the material under scrutiny. There is a real sense in which all theological thinking is circular. That is, as Paul Tillich suggests, any consideration of one theological idea or doctrine implies all the others within the tradition.[7] Since a limited study must be selective, I will try to indicate those theological concepts and concerns which I think are central to establishing a basis for theological criticism of theatre. Specifically, we are concerned here with the biblical concept of creation, and by implication the notion of human creativity, together with the biblical understanding of man as *imago dei*. Beyond this I will try to suggest possible ways in which theology (understood as an articulation of the content and meaning of Christian faith for any age) and art mutually serve each other. As indicated above, the church has never been very clear about this matter, but some guidelines for our inquiry can be set which suggest ways along which mutual and fruitful interpenetration between theology and art may proceed. These matters are taken up in Chapter 1.

As to the material under scrutiny, it is important at the outset to suggest what might be called the theological possibilities in the avant-garde French theatre. This is a matter of the theatre's sensitivities: humanistic, religious, and metaphysical. These sensitivities provide a means for coming to terms with the theatrical tradition out of which the avant-garde French theatre emerges. I will try to indicate that these "theological possibilities" are not imposed upon the French theatre but are germane to it. These matters will be considered in Chapter 2.

The theological judgments concerning a Christian doctrine of man in this study will rely rather heavily upon the insights of Reinhold Niebuhr and his understanding of Christian anthropology. Niebuhr's Gifford Lectures, *The Nature and Destiny of Man*, provide the wellspring of my own theological thinking regarding man, his identity and destiny. As for theological method, I have already indicated an indebtedness to Paul Tillich. He takes his stance within culture where he finds existential questions being asked. Through what he calls a theological analysis of culture, Tillich elucidates the existential questions asked by man's existence and culture and proceeds to correlate these with Christian answers. While I draw certain ideas from the wealth of Tillich's thought, it is not my immediate concern to follow his method in my analysis of the avant-garde French theatre.

I wish to assert at the outset that *theological work is being done in the avant-garde French theatre*, and my purpose is to elucidate this work in terms of the images of man presented in this theatre and compare them with Christian theological understandings. *As theologian I wish to enter into conversation with other theologians who happen to be playwrights by profession.* But I want to note that the questions which will be addressed to the plays considered in this study are indeed questions presupposing a theological answer, though *not necessarily a Christian one.* I am not compelled to correlate questions discerned within culture with my own Christian answers. It is possible to let culture answer in its terms (here, theatrical terms), and this is enough for purposes of conversation.

There has emerged in the past two decades or so an increasing amount of writing which aims at theological criticism of literature.[8] Most of this material addresses itself to the novel and to poetry.[9] The novel, and to a lesser extent poetry, offer themselves to their own kind of didactic purposes, the more subtle and sophisticated the more symbolically expressed. To these purposes a reawakened theological concern with literature readily addresses its own didactic interests, both in contention with what it discerns as anti-Christian and in concert with what it discovers to be secular witness to a sacred truth. The result, however, has been more often a kind of theological imperialism rather than a sensitive probing and listening to what the novelist or poet has to say. I do not wish to follow this procedure which, despite disclaimers by even its more sensitive followers, uses literature as little more than illustrative material to substantiate what is taken to be the continuing relevance of traditional theological and doctrinal concerns.

Central to the concerns of this study is the recognition of the open-endedness of the avant-garde French theatre.

This quality says much about why the theatre has had so little attention from the theological critics of culture. My conclusions about the works discussed are entirely open to question by other serious critics; the more critical and informed opinion, the better. But clearly at stake here is the difficulty of convincing either my fellow theologians, or the playwrights I would engage in conversation, of the legitimacy of the analyses. If I am unable to correlate preconceived doctrinal formulations with the deliverances of the playwrights, my theological brethren are likely to dismiss the enterprise as fruitless. If I appear to abridge the autonomy of the artists for the sake of theological concerns, I am likely to alienate those whose work I most appreciate. Though the way between be a kind of no-man's-land, fraught with pitfalls and obstacles, it is nevertheless an area in need of charting if theologian and playwright are to speak and listen to each other for the sake of the man each of them is and the man they would defend.

THEOLOGY AND ART— A CONCERN

THE CREATED ORDER

Christian theological discourse about art as a distinct and significant human activity properly begins with a theological understanding of creativity. We note both the creative activity of God and the possibilities for creativity within man implied in the doctrine of creation. Theological understanding in this connection stands firmly on biblical testimony, both in the creation myths of Genesis and in the New Testament understanding of Jesus Christ as Son of God and New Adam, through whom God is revealed as Creator-Father.

Central to the biblical understanding of God's creative activity is the distinction between his creative nature and what in fact he has created. To assert that God is creative is to affirm that all his activity is purposeful. To assert that he is the creator of the world is to affirm that what is could not be without him. God is free above his creation, however, and what is could have been otherwise, or not at all.

The concept of God as the Creator precludes both naturalism or spiritualism and mysticism or rationalism. All of these aim to provide man with a world-view which is primarily coherent—so coherent that God himself becomes a part of the universe which is to be explained. God thus becomes either the First Cause or the *Deus ex machina.* By contrast, the privilege of Biblical thought is that in its presentation, the explanation of the universe in its relation to man only serves as a pointer to God—to that without which the explanation could never be constructed, although the explanation does not abrogate the actual inconsistencies of existence.[1]

Thus in the mytho-poetic[2] language of faith God is apprehended as the transcendent creator distinct from his creation, though intimately related to it, and content to pronounce it "good" in its creatureliness.

What is apprehended as God's intimate relationship to creation in the biblical view is not exclusively a matter of his presence before man in personal religious experience. God's creative activity is taken as the origin of history, and history provides the dynamic context for the tripartite relationship: God, man, and world. In this relationship God's purpose in guiding the events of human and world history (regardless of the apparent coherence or incoherence of these events) both roots man and his world in originating creativity and points him beyond himself to an end not contained in history. Otherwise, man and the ambiguities of his existence would not draw their meaning from outside existence, and man would be not a creature, but only some form of being-there, as Martin Heidegger describes him. God not only creates the world; he also sustains it and gives it meaning, both teleological and existential. He gives meaning by giving himself through self-disclosure.

Together with his creatorhood, one of God's primordial attributes in the biblical view is his capacity to reveal himself. In his self-disclosure God reveals himself personally as both judge and loving father in his relationship to man. In his impersonal relationship to the world God is apprehended as the ground of being upon whom all that is depends for its existence. Both these dimensions are held in tension within the idea of relationship, taken by biblical faith to characterize God's creative connection with his creation.[3]

In sum, for biblical faith, God discloses himself to man as the transcendent God who is both hidden and revealed in creation. For Christian faith it is uniquely in Jesus the Christ that God discloses himself historically as creator, sustainer, and redeemer of the world and of men. And this disclosure takes place in the context of fully human and historical relationships of love, judgment, and forgiveness, to which faith attributes the quality of divine perfection. These human relationships are culminated in the cross of Jesus, which faith takes as the symbol of God's own suffering love relationship to his creation. The life and death of Jesus the Christ are finally justified by God in the resurrection event, in which faith discerns God's triumph over death. The end and death of natural man is not the end in the purposes of God. That end is eternal life, an eschatological dimension of God's creativity, which is related to the relationships constituting human existence but not exhausted or fulfilled by them.[4]

FOCUS ON THE *IMAGO DEI*

In the biblical view, man holds a unique place within the created orders. His is both the privilege and the responsibility of dominion over all else that constitutes the created world. The exercise of this dominion is at once man's cultural task and his service to God. The Genesis account of creation formulates man's position in relationship to both God and the world in terms of the concept of the *imago dei*.[5] Man rules the earth not because of his superior intelligence nor because of his natural abilities in other respects, but because he is created in God's image.

Within the concept of the *imago dei* man is seen as a whole being. He is not divided into two separable parts, soul and body. This is an important distinction from other views of man, and particularly in relation to the Greek view, which came to influence a great portion of Christian thought on the meaning of the *imago dei*. As van der Leeuw explains,

> In this regard, that is, anthropologically viewed, there is no difference between the Old and the New Testaments. The latter is just as "primitive" as the former. It is in no way influenced by Greek anthropology, which presupposes the separation between body and soul. For pneuma is not spirit in contrast to body, but divine-holy in contrast to human-sinful life. The entire Platonic differentiation between body and soul is unbiblical.[6]

But van der Leeuw goes on to point out that while both Old and New Testaments affirm the *imago* as an indispensable part of humanity, a shift takes place in which Christ becomes the bearer of the image of God, but it is an image he gives up in order to become the suffering servant, the image of man.

> In Genesis, God creates man after his image and thereby achieves man. In Philippians, God gives up his own form in order to seek out man under his own form, the form of a slave or servant. Here is the heart of the Gospel.
>
> But what has happened, that Paul speaks so differently from the redactor of Genesis? There is no answer in Holy Scripture, neither in Genesis nor elsewhere. But the Church has developed with great assurance from the data of Scripture: the image of God in man is obscured, lost. Between Genesis 1 and Philippians 2 lies the Fall.[7]

The church has wrestled for centuries with the problem of what has happened to the image of God in man so that his existence within history is so manifestly undivine, un-Godlike. This problem must also engage our attention if the concept of the *imago dei* is to be held central for theological criticism of literature.

The Christian tradition encompasses two major approaches to the question of the image of God in relation to the fall. One has been the Christological approach in which the specifically Christian revelation has been taken as normative and the concepts of *imago dei*, creation, and fall have been understood in the light of it. The other has been an essentially anthropological approach in which an effort has been made to secure the natural endowments of man while maintaining the religious assertion that man stands in need of salvation. This second approach largely dominated the tradition through the Scholastic period and up to the Reformation.

What we are here calling the anthropological approach to the fall is a natural theology which proceeds upon the assumption that there can be a differentiation between the two terms of what Genesis calls the "image and likeness" of God in created man. Modern biblical studies clearly show that no such distinction can be made on the basis of the biblical texts alone. But several of the early church fathers did make such a distinction. Its essence lies in grouping universal human characteristics (reason, freedom, human form) under the image and grouping religious characteristics (immortal life, moral equality with God, communion with God) under the likeness. The result is a two-story notion of man, the upper story (likeness) destroyed in the fall, and the bottom story (image) remaining intact. In this view, the work of Christ is the restoration of the upper story.

This is precisely the distinction which the Scholastics fastened upon for the full development of medieval Christian anthropology. Clearly the church was aware of the necessity of proclaiming the fall of man and its consequences regarding his condition in relation to God. But the church said far more than can be supported by biblical testimony or that can avoid all the unfortunate results of dualism, which have continued to set such an orientation at odds both with man's rootedness in the world and with his capacity for self-transcendence.

The thought of the Reformers was only partially helpful. For instance, while Calvin resolutely rejected the differentiation between image and likeness and thus saw the whole man as the image of God, he yet declared that the image was radically distorted. "Wherefore, although we grant that the image of God was not utterly effaced and destroyed in [Adam], it was, however, so corrupted, that any thing which remains is fearful deformity . . ."[8] To say the least, within such a framework it is difficult to locate the man who became the instrument of the incarnation. If the Eastern church (with its surer sense that the concept of the *imago dei* must lead to the realization "that God, in his revelation to man, has a face"[9]) tends toward an apotheosis of man, the Western church in its iconoclasm leads to the kind of philosophical assertion in which man is merely being-there. In any case, the anthropological approach to the fall renders the assertion that the image of God remains in man and remains meaningful to man's self-understanding, problematic indeed.

The Christological approach to the meaning of the fall and the continuing significance of the *imago dei* comes at the problem from a different perspective. Karl Barth is instructive at this point, even though we are not obliged to go all the way with him in his Christocentrism. Barth has forcefully reminded us that for Christian faith knowledge of God as creator and of man as image of God is only appropriated through the revelation of Christ. As we have already noted, the Old Testament concept of the image residing in man is shifted in the New Testament to where Christ is the bearer of both the image of God and the true image of man. Thus, in Christian faith, anthropology follows from Christology. The issue centers in the relationship between the *image of God* and the *image of the servant*. In the Christian testimony Christ willingly gave up the image of God in order to fully become the image of the servant. And the full significance of this image is revealed in the cross of Jesus. For Christian faith it is fallen man with whom Christ identifies in the incarnation, and for this man the image of God is not a possibility, only the image of the servant. Regardless of what natural powers and possibilities philosophical anthropology may discover in man, Christian anthropology speaks of man's need for a new creation which will once more restore the image of God to him. This restoration is a matter of reconciliation with God through the faithful obedience of Jesus the Christ, the image of the servant.

In Christian faith what is restored to man is not moral equality with God nor immortality nor even automatic fellowship with him, but the possibility of faith. That is, in Christ is revealed the true image for man, which is the image of the servant, and restored to man is the possibility of faithful response to this image, this form. In this understanding, faith becomes obedience to the image, the form, not some belief in a scientifically unsupportable idea or theory. In faithful obedience to the image of the servant, the Christian lives his life in society as well as in the community of faith, the church.

In this simple obedience lies what a secularized Christianity is wont to call its "cultural task," and concerning which it asks with alternating distaste and appetite to what degree it must or may be able to fulfill this task. This cultural task is in reality the obedience of faith, and it is fulfilled where we recognize the form of God's creation and adapt ourselves to it. Here we find the possibility and the reality of art, whose nature is form; but here we also find the possibility and the reality of the Christian life in the broadest sense of the word. It is the setting of faith in worship and liturgy, in the order of state and society, in the entire "service" which God demands of us, by desiring to become "of like form with the image of his Son."[10]

The Genesis account says nothing of the loss of the image of God, and yet the whole biblical testimony from Genesis to Philippians can be read as a narrative response to this loss. Christian faith asserts that the image of God appears again in history in Jesus Christ, but that this image has now been emptied of glory and has assumed the form of "the man of sorrows."

It is important to notice that the Christological approach to the *imago dei* and its restoration avoids the temptation to both angelism and total depravity as definitive understandings of man. The Christian faith is concerned with the whole man. And it is the whole man who is called to obedience to the image of the servant through faith in Jesus Christ.

In this connection, it is also important to note the Deuteronomic proscription of image making. The issue is the one great sin, idolatry. While the imaginative life is nothing but image making, it is something else to assert in puritanical fashion that all image making (i.e., all art) is idolatrous. Image making becomes idolatrous either when the images we make are taken for ultimate reality or when we try to manipulate, for our own ends, the one great image given to us, the image of the servant. The image of the servant is a concrete, living image that can only be shared in, participated in, represented in living form in the lives of men.

It is interesting, further, to note that from Xenophanes to Feuerbach and Freud there has been a line of thought in the West which appears to take with radical seriousness the proscription against image making, whether heard from the lips of the Deuteronomist or not. The repeated assertion has been that man has made God after his own image. The charge is always that men are guilty of the sin of idolatry, the anthropomorphous projection of themselves (in either their best or worst moments) into the realm of deity. This charge needs to be taken seriously, but equally serious is the covert denial of the living God underlying the charge as it comes from many of its most articulate enthusiasts. While anthropomorphic language is unavoidable in the human attempt to articulate God's self-disclosure to faith, because of the incarnation the Christian does not hesitate here. Insofar as man offers his own image *to* God, not *as* God, the man of faith is not defeated by charges of anthropomorphism, since God himself chose to present himself in human form. "In the form of the crucified, humiliated and problematic, yet eternally worthy of worship, lies a judgment, but at the same time also a justification, for all human attempts at creating form."[11]

CHRISTIAN ANTI-HUMANISM

With the suggestion that in the *image of the servant* lies both a judgment upon and justification for human creative and imaginative activity, we come upon an extension of the problem which the Christian tradition has had in dealing with man as *imago dei*. We have noted that the anthropological approach to the issue has always tended to divide man into two parts, one natural and the other fallen and in need of redemption. The overwhelming tendency within the tradition has been to deprecate human existence and human possibilities in the light of this division. Too often, man as sinful has been identified with man as finite, but we have noted that in the biblical view man as finite creature is not sinful because his life is bound up with a body that dies. Rather, man is fallen because in sinful pride he places himself into the center of reality, thus usurping the place of God.

When, however, the church has identified sinfulness with finitude or with the body and its rootedness in the world, it has also tended to extend this identification to man's imaginative activity. Always ready to be drawn into service has been the commandment concerning image making. It is not by chance, therefore, that when a Greek tradition of the arts, with its aesthetic and poetics of life-imitation, came into contact with an iconoclastic Christianity, the imaginative life became the loser. From Tertullian's famous question, "What has Athens to do with Jerusalem?" to Abelard's similar question, "What has Horace to do with the Psalter, Virgil with the Gospel, Cicero with the Apostle?"[12] we can delineate a tradition that has held suspect all human imaginative life that did not conform with the most rigorous adherence to the letter of the biblical and dogmatic traditions. Even in the eighteenth century, an age generally quite confident about man and his possibilities, we find Alexander Pope saying that man is "In doubt to deem himself a god, or beast, / In doubt his mind or body to prefer; / Born but to die, and reas'ning but to err."[13]

Unfortunately, the tradition of Christian anti-humanism continues to the present time. Its more virulent forms are evident in both fundamentalist Protestant thought and in spiritualist Roman Catholic assertion. Whenever this life is seen fundamentally as a preparation for an otherwordly existence, historical human reality becomes degraded. The literary manifestations of this fundamentalist viewpoint are of little consequence theologically and of less creative merit. There are, however, more subtle forms of the tradition expressed in imaginative literature. These will be noted below in the section on art as a resource for theology.

CHRISTIAN HUMANISM

Parallel to Christian anti-humanism, and even in some thinkers overlapping it, lies the tradition of Christian humanism. What is meant by "Christian humanism" is the serious and dedicated concern of Christian thinkers with the relation-

ships between theology and culture in its broader manifestations. What is meant here is not a philosophy of humanism which begins and ends with natural man nor a refraction
of cultural achievement through the prism of Christian dog-
mas, but a genuine appreciation of art and culture as gifts of
the spirit.

> The depth, strength, and diversity of the tradition of Chris-
> tian humanism may best be defined by recalling that it in-
> cludes Augustine, Dante, Erasmus, Zwingli, Melanchthon,
> Calvin, Sir Philip Sidney, John Milton, and Dr. Samuel John-
> son, to name only a few.[14]

When recalling the Reformers, one is more often reminded of
the frightful picture of Luther's followers smashing stained
glass windows in churches, pane by pane. And yet we find
Luther writing to a friend:

> I am persuaded that without knowledge of literature pure
> theology cannot at all endure, just as heretofore, when letters
> have declined and lain prostrate, theology, too, has wretchedly
> fallen and lain prostrate; nay, I see that there has never been
> a great revelation of the Word of God unless He has first
> prepared the way by the rise and prosperity of languages and
> letters, as though they were John the Baptists. . . . Certainly
> it is my desire that there shall be as many poets and rhetori-
> cians as possible, because I see that by these studies, as by no
> other means, people are wonderfully fitted for the grasping of
> sacred truth and for handling it skillfully and happily.[15]

Even Calvin, whose pronouncements concerning human possibilities are not overly optimistic, can say,

> Therefore, in reading profane authors, the admirable light
> of truth displayed in them should remind us, that the human
> mind, however much fallen and perverted from its original
> integrity, is still adorned and invested with admirable gifts
> from its Creator. If we reflect that the Spirit of God is the
> only fountain of truth, we will be careful, as we would avoid
> offering insult to him, not to reject or contemn truth wher-

ever it appears. In despising the gifts, we insult the Giver.
... Therefore, since it is manifest that men whom the Scrip-
tures term natural, are so acute and clear-sighted in the in-
vestigation of inferior things, their example should teach us
how many gifts the Lord has left in possession of human
nature, notwithstanding of its having been despoiled of the
true good.[16]

But it is one thing to attribute man's art and science to
the inspiration of God and another to assert that man's
cultural greatness provides grounds for either self-satisfaction
or assurance of salvation. This latter assertion the Reformers
did not make; cultural achievement is neither sacerdotal nor
soteriological in function, regardless of how significant it
may be for the full expression and appreciation of human
existence. Perhaps Pascal speaks a definitive word when he
says,

> The greatness of man is great in that he knows himself to be
> miserable. A tree does not know itself to be miserable. It is
> then being miserable to know oneself to be miserable; but it is
> also being great to know that one is miserable. All these same
> miseries prove man's greatness. They are the miseries of a
> great lord, of a deposed king.[17]

Such misery can never be simply a matter of deprivation of
this world's securities, important as these are to general human
welfare. Rather, the misery of which Pascal speaks points to
that primal deprivation of the *imago dei*, the knowledge of
which deprivation constitutes greatness, whether it be perceived in Israel's history, Oedipus' pride, or King Lear's
despair and madness. In *Prometheus Bound*, Aeschylus has
Hermes speak the following remarkable lines to Prometheus:

> Look for no ending to this agony
> Until a god will freely suffer for you,
> Will take on him your pain, and in your stead
> Descend to where the sun is turned to darkness,

The black depths of death.
Take thought: this is no empty boast
But utter truth.[18]

Christian faith answers Hermes with the assertion that indeed God incarnate in Jesus the Christ has accomplished this suffering on our behalf. The Christian complement to Aeschylus' lines is the Apostles' Creed.

Within a framework of Christian humanism which seeks to understand and appreciate the insights of art and science into man's situation and condition and appropriate these for a more adequate theology, the present study seeks to take its place. Important here is the admission that theology is no less the work of cultural man than is painting or statecraft. The theologian believes that the same God judges both artist and theologian. Whether the artist shares this belief is not so important as the theologian's recognition that God may be speaking more meaningfully through the artist than through the theologian. This bare possibility alone is sufficient rationale for the present study, though our method must be to listen to the artist in his own terms and let conversation proceed from that point.

HUMAN CREATIVITY

What in human creativity opens the man of letters to theological analysis at the very center of his art? The poet (from the Green *poiein*, to make), is not simply a manipulator of words, versifier, but one who makes, a creator, one who fashions materials at hand into something new, a created good. In the classical tradition the poet was a maker who imitated the natural world (variously though this world be understood). Irving Babbitt, in his essay, "On Being Creative," cites the emergence of the phrase "creative imagination" as indicative of the turn in modern times from the tradition of imitation toward mere novelty. "A boundless intoxication with novelty is indeed the outstanding trait of the modern era that sets it off from all the ages of the past."[19] Babbitt credits the marvelous deliverances of the natural sciences as the source of the jealousy which has led men of letters to fasten upon the creative imagination in its bent toward novelty, thus providing a "me too" stance for the poets vis-à-vis creativity. Babbitt's famous pupil, T. S. Eliot, together with a well-known list of critics (Allen Tate, John Crowe Ransom, R. P. Blackmur, and others), has taken with genuine seriousness the threat of the sciences to reduce all meaningful discourse to propositional language. These men have both appreciated Babbitt's urging toward the classical tradition of imitation and sought to secure for poetry a truly cognitive function within the broad scope of human imagination. While the gains in the latter effort have been impressive for purposes of understanding literature in its own terms, there has been a tendency to cut literature off from the broader world beyond its own stylistic and syntactical boundaries. Nathan A. Scott, Jr., summarized the achievement of modern literary criticism in the following way:

> The fully achieved work of art, as the argument runs, is a discrete and closed system of mutually interrelated terms: the organic character of the structure prevents the constituent terms from being atomistically wrenched out of their context and made to perform a simple referential function, and it also succeeds in so segregating the total structure from the circumambient world as to prevent its entering into an extramural affiliation. "A poem should not mean but be," says Mr. MacLeish, and thereby, in this famous line from his poem "Ars Poetica," he summarizes, with a beautiful concision, the mind of a generation.[20]

The splendid ontological autonomy which this kind of criticism grants to the work of art makes any statement about it very difficult, thus undercutting the critical task itself. Allen Tate has expressed this difficulty in his agonized question, "is literary criticism possible?"[21] Scott suggests that this problem arises from an inadequate understanding of the creative process itself. The major literary theorists of our time have declared, often quite mystically, that language itself brings meaning into existence. No doubt language is of inestimable importance in understanding what about poetry is genuinely creative, but the words themselves, either singly or in combination, never point only inward to the context. Words have, as Scott says, an "incorrigibly referential thrust"[22] beyond themselves to the world. This is a way of suggesting that literary art transcends its own stylistic and syntactical boundaries.

We need to be careful here lest we fall into another version of the words-bring-meaning-to-birth theory of R. P. Blackmur. It is not the words which contain "the meaning as an imminent possibility before the pangs of junction."[23] Rather, it is a matter of how the poet (or playwright) in his own "creative intuition" orients the statement toward the world which grants transcendence to the work of art. Denis de Rougemont is helpful in this connection when he says,

> Whether it consists in a structure of meanings, or forms, or sounds, or ideas, the work of art has for its specific function the bribing of the attention, the magnetizing of the sensibility, the fascinating of the meditation, the ensnaring—and at the same time it must orient existence toward something which transcends sounds and forms, or the words so assembled. It is a trap, but an oriented trap.[24]

Scott is convinced that we can link this orienting of the work of art toward the world with the beliefs of the artist, which, in turn, come to bear upon the creative process itself.

The phrase "creative intuition" is used by Jacques Maritain to denote the creative act as described in his book, *Creative Intuition in Art and Poetry*. Scott adduces Maritain's understanding of the creative act because within Maritain's thinking the whole self of the artist (including his beliefs) is brought into play in the creative act, and this understanding helps us see the importance of the artist's beliefs in his own vision of the world. We are not dealing here with a self-conscious system of belief, the kind of "thinking" which T. S. Eliot considers unimportant to the creative act. For Maritain, the artist's creative intuition is "an obscure grasping of his own Self and of things in a knowledge through union or through connaturality which is born in the spiritual unconscious, and which fructifies only in the work."[25] The creative intuition grasps

> some complex of concrete and individual reality, . . . the singular existent which resounds in the subjectivity of the poet, together with all the other realities which echo in this existent, and which it conveys in the manner of a sign.[26]

The poetic statement, then, becomes a sign, or expression, of how the poet in his own "interiority" and vision grasps the world and gives it order and meaning. Maritain opens up to us "a stratagem for declaring once again that it is not language which brings 'meaning to birth' and which enables the mind 'to order itself'—not language, but *vision*."[27]

In summary, we can say that while modern literary theorists have granted us a renewed sense of the importance of the literary work itself, they have undercut their own critical task by isolating the work of art both from the artist's own vision and from the surrounding world. By noting both the transcendent dimension of art as well as the significance of the artist's beliefs in the creative act, we are enabled to affirm that language plus vision control the creative act. The vision must be discerned in the work itself, and critical assessment of how the writer employs language will elucidate it. Therefore, we must always look to the work itself, but do so in the recognition that the work bears testimony both to the writer's vision and to the surrounding world of which it is a part.

In light of the foregoing, the Christian critic is enabled to affirm that man as creature is capable of genuine creation, but that the artist, from a Christian perspective, is subject to the image of man as servant both in himself and in the images of man he creates. This study will be concerned with such images as literary and dramatic creations.

ART AS A RESOURCE FOR THEOLOGY

We have been using the term "art" in both a general and a specific sense. We must now limit ourselves to the specific sense of literary art and to drama as a dimension of this art. In the next chapter we will be discussing some of the ways in which theatre, as an art encompassing drama and giving it location in time and space, adds to what can now be said about the interpenetration of literature and theology. We are limited by the paucity of critical studies that have sought to relate theatre to theology. Drama, particularly tragic drama, has been given considerable attention in connection with poetry and the novel, but in all this the written literature as distinct in important ways from theatre has engaged the attention of critics, both Christian and non-Christian. For instance, Roland M. Frye suggests a program for the Christian critic in the following way:

> Literature may be related to the Christian faith in three ways: first, as literary method in the use of symbol, metaphor, and story is applicable to the understanding of Biblical truth; second, as literature treats, in basic and universal terms, both the affirmations and the problems of human existence with which theology must come to grips; and last, as specific writers express their visions of life in terms of a Christian frame of reference.[28]

The second of Frye's proposals comes closest to the purposes of the present study. However, within such a method of relating literature to theology there are both assumptions and problems which need elucidating.

The assumption that only literature dealing with universal human affirmations and problems is appropriate for Christian criticism would seem to imply both too much and too little about theology. The problem is with the doctrines of creation and incarnation. To speak of universal human affirmations and problems implies that theology must await the deliverances of speculative philosophy as to human universals, on the one hand, which is saying too much. And to speak thus underestimates the significance of particularity in human existence and history, on the other hand, which is not saying enough. William F. Lynch, S. J., is particularly helpful in this connection in his book *Christ and Apollo* when he focuses the attention of the Christian critic on the particularity of finite existence. In speaking of the images of finitude which daily confront us in existence, Father Lynch says,

> My own attitude toward these images of limitation . . . is that the images are in themselves the path to whatever the self is seeking: to insight, or beauty, or, for that matter, to God. This path is both narrow and direct; it leads, I believe, straight through our human realities, through our labor, our disappointments, our friends, our game legs, our harvests, our subjection to time. There are no shortcuts to beauty or to insight. We must go *through* the finite, the limited, the definite, omitting none of it lest we omit some of the potencies of being-in-the-flesh.[29]

As Father Lynch goes on to point out, not all literature takes this kind of view toward the finite realities of the created order. We may say here that the literature which does point us toward the reality of the finite is of particular help to theology as theology tries to articulate for the present age the significance of the doctrines of creation and incarnation. Such art is a genuine resource for theology as it puts in imaginative images the concrete contingencies of human existence.

Yet it is just here that another problem is encountered: the disparagement of concrete human existence. We have already noted the seemingly ineradicable stream of such disparagement in Christian thought. Even so great an appreciator of culture and art as Jacques Maritain is placed in this stream by Gabriel Vahanian:

> Maritain's positive approach to the independent reality of culture is but a pretext better to absorb it into the realm of an otherworldly reality, namely the Christian tradition. . . . All that Maritain's theory of aesthetics, all that his religious philosophy of culture, achieves is to reassert, even if mildly, the old deprecation of life here on earth.[30]

While this is no doubt not the last word on Maritain, it does point up the subtle temptation within even the most rigorous of Christian thinkers to point men away from the world rather than to it. But this problem does not belong only to Christian thought.

Nathan A. Scott, Jr., delineates within modern Western literature a similar life-denying stream of sensibility. What he calls "an experiment in angelism" within modern letters has produced a literature of escape which is associated with many of the greatest names of the period. This effort to escape the realities of finite existence has been pursued "through magical *gnosis*, through withdrawal into *la poésie pure*, or into the light and airy realms of pure sensibility, or, finally, into the inebriation of *Angst*.[31] The line runs from Lautréamont and Baudelaire to Sartre and Camus.

THEOLOGY AS INTERPRETER OF ART

To the extent that life-affirmation, including its ambiguities and contingencies, is a problem for literature as well as for Christian thought, literature provides a warning which theology must heed if its own affirmations concerning the created order are to speak with sensitivity to the imaginative prehensions of reality which literature delivers. On the other hand, precisely because life-denial is not the only word which Christian theology has to offer to man-in-existence, there is the possibility of theology offering something necessary to literature. As Professor Amos N. Wilder and others[32] have ably demonstrated, the biblical tradition holds central within its witness a life affirmation.

> Revelation and the grace of God are tied up inseparably with our "somatic" existence, as we say today; that is, with our fleshly-sensuous-bodily life with all its organic relationships, widening out as these do into the social, economic and political spheres. God does not and cannot by-pass the original endowment with which he created us; nor the bonds that link us with nature, family and clan. Any understanding of Christ or of the early church or of the theology of Paul or of the message for today which disassociates these from man's natural affections and common needs is bound to be wrong. Any redemption so offered us will not be a truly relevant one.[33]

In pointing to the this-wordly aspect of the biblical understanding of existence, Wilder also relates the modern misunderstanding of this emphasis to the kind of modern art which Scott calls "an experiment in angelism." The point is well made by Wilder when he insists that both theology and art must address the whole man.

> Christianity like modern art must take its materials from the stuff of life, ugly and dangerous though much of it is. . . . T. S. Eliot's great achievement rests on the fact that he has himself been initiated into the furies and stagnations of our age and its cities. The language of Eliot is not an idealist language. It is not, fortunately, an angelic, an uncontaminated, an immaculate language. Both the artist and his language have to be baptized in reality if they are to be effective.[34]

Because the doctrines of creation and incarnation articulate for faith a "baptism in reality," theology has something to offer to literature. How this can best be achieved is perhaps open to wide questioning. The present effort is by analyzing alternative images of man.

THEOLOGICAL POSSIBILITIES
IN THE AVANT-GARDE FRENCH THEATRE—
A MATTER OF SENSITIVITIES

To suggest that there are genuine possibilities for theological criticism of the avant-garde French theatre of the 1950's is in no sense to assert that this theatre is concerned with presenting religious drama. We are not concerned here with a Paul Claudel, important a playwright as he was.[1] His kind of theatre is indeed rich in religious symbolism and is clearly oriented by his theological perspective. Our concern lies with a self-consciously non-Catholic modern French theatre which nevertheless lends itself to theological criticism. We are not concerned with doctrine: we are concerned with sensitivities that open onto theological discussion. We may call these sensitivities humanistic, religious, and metaphysical. The humanistic sensitivities bespeak man's predicament as man; the religious sensitivities bespeak the kind and quality of man's relationships; the metaphysical sensitivities bespeak the nature of man's world.

HUMANISTIC SENSITIVITIES

That modern man lives in a radically distempered age is no longer a new suggestion. In spite of social-scientific analyses concerning the "lonely crowd" and "organization man," the ascendent sign of the age is what we have come to call "the death of God." Although Nietzsche did not initiate the movement within modern sensibility, he did fix its form in *Thus Spoke Zarathustra*.[2] This was 1883. Prior to Nietzsche, Hölderlin had been speaking of the need for the poet to name the gods who, "it is true, are living,/Yet far above ourselves, away in a different world."[3] And subsequent to Nietzsche the poet Rilke said in a letter to Ilse Jahr that "attributes are taken away from God, the no longer expressible, fall back to creation, to love and death . . ."[4] That the sign of the age had finally reached the sensibility of the general populace was graphically disclosed in Jean-Paul Sartre's "laconic salutation in an address to newspapermen gathered in Geneva after [World War II]: 'Gentlemen, God is dead.' "[5]

Contrary to Nietzsche's expectation, the birth of the *übermensch* did not accompany the death of God. Rather with the death of God has come in many ways the death of man. To be sure, the existentialist movement in both philosophy and literature has called modern man to an affirmation of authentic existence through engagement in the common life, without illusions, without absolutes, without God. But alongside existentialism has persisted the theme of the loss of both man and God. If man is not yet dead to his own humanity, he has nevertheless become a victim of the corrosive acids of modern existence until he is nameless and faceless, the user of a language which does not communicate, the possessor of a body in which he stands in guilt and isolation. Man without God has become man in peril of losing his humanity. Such is modern man's predicament.

Under the sign of the death of God our age has lost its hold on all certainties of value and conduct which an earlier age guaranteed by absolute precepts deduced from an absolute God. In this situation the avant-garde theatre in France has emerged as a powerful reminder that despite the loss of absolute norms for human existence man is yet faced with an ultimate situation. This theatre is not interested in arguing philosophically concerning man's condition. This was the stance taken by existentialist theatre as practiced by Camus and especially Sartre. The avant-garde theatre presents modern man in the situation in which he is faced with the loss of his humanity. Martin Esslin is convinced that this presentation becomes, paradoxically, a kind of religious quest, a search for a "dimension of the Ineffable." For Esslin this search becomes

> an effort to make man aware of the ultimate realities of his condition, to instill in him again the lost sense of cosmic wonder and primeval anguish, to shock him out of an existence that has become trite, mechanical, complacent, and deprived of the dignity that comes of awareness.[6]

Arthur Adamov, one of the playwrights to be discussed, wrote a kind of confessional account of his own inner awareness called L'Aveu. In a portion of this work, translated as "The Endless Humiliation," Adamov speaks of his own sense of separation at the source of his being. In answer to the question, From what are you separated?, Adamov answers in his interior dialogue:

> All I know is that I am suffering, and that if I am suffering it is because at the source of myself there is mutilation, separation. I do not know what name to give what I am separated from, but I am separated from it. Once it was called God. Now there is no longer any name.[7]

Adamov's conclusion is that all men are similarly separated, alienated, and hence are guilty in their isolation.

Under the sign of the death of God and with an awareness of the inner separation and alienation of modern man, the avant-garde theatre becomes a mirror of the victimized state of man without God. One method of presenting this man is the use of language which sounds commonsensical but in which communication does not occur. At best the language which man uses reveals his private anxieties and neuroses, but such revelations are surrealistic, dreamlike, rather than rational. Hence not only does communication become a problem for modern man, but failure at communication becomes a sign of man's victimized state. Other indications of man's situation revealed in this theatre are his failure at meaningful relationships, his inability to use time significantly, and his inability to resist the crushing weight of a material universe. Without God man becomes a victim of himself, his fellowman, and his world. Such a situation we may justly call the predicament of the threat of the loss of humanity.

In response to this situation theology has something to say both about the silence and hiddenness of God and about a quality of human life which overcomes separation and alienation. It must be noted, however, that the avant-garde theatre *does not discuss* the death of God; this is assumed.[8] But also assumed is that man has a world which transcends him and is not simply a projection of his ego. The dimension of transcendence is thus important for this theatre, and it is expressed in both the spatial metaphors of depth and the beyond. With respect to this dimension of transcendence theology finds an opening for what may be said about God's absence and man's victimized state.

RELIGIOUS SENSITIVITIES

Clearly what we have been discussing as humanistic sensitivities of the contemporary French theatre contain implications for both religious and metaphysical sensitivities. To define religious sensitivities in terms of human relationships is warranted by a biblical understanding of religion and by the attempt which the avant-garde theatre has made to reconstitute human relationships in terms of communion. We need to be careful here to note that what is presented on the stage is an image of man for whom communication is problematic, but in this presentation a communicative relationship is sought between actor and audience, which can only be described as communion. Because communication has broken down in the modern world and because the communion of the Mass no longer speaks to man's condition, the theatre seeks to fill the vacuum.

The avant-garde theatre stands in a modern tradition identified with the work of Alfred Jarry in the late nineteenth century, with Guillaume Apollinaire and the Surrealist movement of the early twentieth century, and particularly with the inspirational influence of Antonin Artaud and his manifestos on a new concept of the theatre, gathered under the title *The Theatre and Its Double*. Some men within this tradition such as Jacques Copeau and Henri Gheon, themselves Roman Catholics, sought to establish a one-to-one analogous relationship between the participants of the Mass and the participants in theatre. In general, the concept for these men is that the play represents the sanctified host, the playwright represents the priest, and the audience represents the congregation of the faithful.[9] The avant-garde playwrights are less interested in this kind of strict analogy than they are in creating a theatre in which communication takes place between actor and audience below the surface of ordinary relationships. Communion in this context does not consist in identifying the audience with what is going on on the stage. Quite the opposite is intended. By distorting language and gesture, by pushing all the elements of rational discourse to the breaking point, this theatre aims at raising the question of communication and relationships in such a shocking and forceful fashion that the members of the audience cannot help but open up to new depths within themselves. By its being made unmistakably clear that what is taking place on the stage is an illusion, the illusory character of ordinary relationships outside the theatre is revealed. It takes the actors and the audience together to make the revelation present, and at this level a new kind of communion takes place.

We are not concerned here with togetherness for its own sake. The theatre does not aim at collective experience. The modern world provides a surfeit of collectives in which all men participate, though generally without commitment. Erich Kahler, in his book *Man the Measure*, says this about modern man and his collectivized experience:

> ... the average individual of a modern metropolis is no longer a real person. He is a focus, an intersection point of various collective interests, collective activities, collective inclinations and reactions. His personality consists almost wholly of the specific combination of collective interests that meet within him.[10]

Such a man is in need of communal experience which will relate him to his fellowman at the spiritual level of the hopes, frustrations, aspirations, and sensibilities shared by all men. Even the churches are collectives in modern society, or at least they tend to be when social mobility, coupled with the demise of ethnic subcultures, undercuts both social and theological traditions. The "community" church has become the religious expression of a pluralistic society in which religiosity is traded for commitment. And yet a deeply felt need for community remains, and the modern theatre has sought to speak to this need.

It would be overstating the case to suggest that the avant-garde theatre has sought to provide an experience of communion and a tangible expression of community on the basis of any sustained body of theory. We are dealing here with what we have called a religious sensitivity. The ideas of Copeau and Gheon have influenced some of the actor-directors responsible for mounting productions of the avant-garde plays, but the more direct influence on the playwrights themselves has been Antonin Artaud. Artaud's concept of a total theatre which seeks to establish communion at the level of dream images and preconscious psychic experience was never completely worked out, and his own efforts to create a theatre to match his concept was a notable failure.[11] Yet within the failure was an inspiration to the avant-garde playwrights who, in highly individual and personal ways, have sought to communicate personal visions of reality which gain at least some of their theatrical warrant from Artaud's insights.

In the case of each playwright we will be discussing, the effort has been to create a theatre of participation in which the audience is involved in both conscious and unconscious ways. The avant-gardists have compromised between Artaud's call for a nonliterary, essentially anti-conscious, theatre and what Bertold Brecht called an effect of "alienation." The result is a theatre which seeks to shock the audience into an awareness of existence beyond, beneath, above, behind, within, outside the strictures of everyday bourgeois life; and this is achieved through poetic images which speak both to pre-conscious levels and to highly conscious and, theatrically speaking, "alienated" levels of the audience's awareness and experience. Thus an attempt is made to return the theatre to something of its original religious function wherein man is faced with his personal, social, and cosmic situation through poetic images made of language and gesture, music and dance, sound and sight. This becomes a "mytho-poetic theatre."

As we saw in Chapter 1, biblical faith and theological reflection upon it have a stake in mytho-poetic visions of man and the significance of these for human self-understanding. In the Judeo-Christian tradition man is understood as person, an individual within community. This community has the horizontal dimensions of human brotherhood in general and historical communities in particular. It also has the vertical dimension of communion with God. While the church has often been too quick to cry paganism or heresy upon communities based upon spurious spiritual values, we have only to remember Nazism to find the kind of point at which Christian awareness of basically anti-human communities becomes relevant. At the same time, the sensitivity for community and communion, and their lack, which we have been noting in the modern theatre, arises in no small part out of the manifest failure of the church as institution and dogmatic tradition to speak meaningfully to the masses of modern men. There is need here for mutual interpenetration of theatre and theology. It is commonplace that art becomes a surrogate religion for many individuals and particularly for practicing artists. It is another matter when both the theatre and the church as social institutions claim to provide the kind of communion which relates persons to one another at the level of fundamental human reality. Insofar as both claim to be valid religious institutions, such claims need discussion and possibly judgment in the name of man himself.

METAPHYSICAL SENSITIVITIES

We have seen how the humanistic sensitivities of the avant-garde theatre have led the playwrights to present their images of modern man in a theatre that has the quality of communion about it. Thus humanistic sensitivities have led to religious sensitivities. There is yet a third sensitivity inextricably bound up with the others. It may be called the metaphysical sensitivity which bespeaks man's world. Just as the depiction of modern man in this theatre takes place in an event binding actors and audience together into one whole act, so this act takes place within both a physical and a metaphysical context. And these two contexts are not to be separated.

We have already mentioned Antonin Artaud. His influence upon the avant-garde theatre is most persuasive in this matter of metaphysical sensitivities. In reaction to stage realism and psychologism, to the commercial theatre, and to the tradition of literary theatre, Artaud set about to undermine

what he felt to be a decadent theatre and to do so by
developing a "theatre of cruelty." "We are not free," Artaud
insisted, "and the sky can still fall on our heads. And the
theatre has been created to teach us that first of all."[12]
Man's situation is precarious in the world, and what is
needed is the kind of theatre which will remind us that there
are dangers and depths to existence which are not encompassed by our rational, conscious, and bourgeois habits
of living. Such a reminder will of necessity be something of a
dislocation from our habitual patterns of life and thus a cruel
reminder. In Oriental theatre, especially the Balinese theatre,
Artaud found his inspiration for a theatre which speaks at
levels below the customary Western terms of discourse. From
this non-Western theatre he drew his basic ideas of a metaphysical theatre that would once more become "reconciled"
with the universe which is shut off to us in our Western
ways.

To free what is truly theatrical about the theatre, Artaud
felt that the tyranny of language must be broken. Once this
is accomplished we will be in position to realize that "the
stage is a concrete physical place which asks to be filled, and
to be given its own concrete language to speak."[13] Needed
is "a poetry of the senses," a "concrete physical language"
which "is truly theatrical only to the degree that the thoughts
it expresses are beyond the reach of the spoken language."[14]
Such a language would consist of the "aspects of all the
means of expression utilizable on the stage, such as music,
dance, plastic art, pantomime, mimicry, gesticulation, in-
tonation, architecture, lighting, and scenery."[15] In other
words, the *mise en scène* must be brought to the fore. Too
often the elements of theatre composing the *mise en scène*
are relegated to a secondary position, that necessary "craft"
which is basic but not finally significant in ordinary, literary
theatre. Artaud bitterly attacks such a denegation of the
mise en scène when he says,

> . . . a theater which subordinates the *mise en scène* and pro-
> duction, i.e., everything in itself that is specifically theatrical,
> to the text, is a theater of idiots, madmen, inverts, grammarians,
> grocers, anti-poets and positivists, i.e., Occidentals.[16]

Such a theatre, preoccupied with the solutions to psychological
and social problems, reeks of "*carrion man.*" What is needed
is "a little breath of that great metaphysical fear which is at
the root of all ancient theater."[17]

Through manipulation of the *mise en scène* Artaud hoped
to produce a genuinely metaphysical theatre which would
relate men to the primal world of forces and powers beyond
the surface experience of life.

> Everything in this active poetic mode of envisaging ex-
> pression on the stage leads us to abandon the modern human-
> istic and psychological meaning of the theater, in order to
> recover the religious and mystic preference of which our the-
> ater has completely lost the sense.[18]

In such a theatre, language would become incantation, and
the physical space of the theatre would be filled with a
concrete language of movement, objects, light, and sound
which, together with incantatory language, would, through
shock and violence and blood if necessary, cause us to once
more become "like victims burnt at the stake, signaling through
the flames."[19]

A martyr image no doubt overstates the case for what
is needed to reorient the theatre toward the depths of experience, depths which can only be described as metaphysical.
But Artaud's call for a theatre in which the total skill and
equipment of the theatre participates in ultimate reality does
bear attention. Insofar as such a theatre is possible, both man
and his world are encompassed in a complex poetic image
which carries significance quite beyond the more customary
theatrical discourse about man and his problems. Such a
theatre does not tell us about man's condition personally,
socially, and metaphysically; it presents man in his situation,

and we, the audience, are part of that total situation as are the four walls of the building in which the theatrical event takes place. Such a theatre cannot be understood in terms of an Ibsenesque stage—a drawing room with a wall removed so that action can be observed and discourse heard. Such a metaphysical theatre aims at a holistic experience in which actors and audience in communion are once again related to a universe which is transcendent to the logic and consciousness of any single participant, or indeed to all the parties collectively. In their differing ways, the avant-garde playwrights follow Artaud's lead here.

> Artaud's major contribution, then, would seem to lie not so much in form itself, but in a basic intention: a theatre of shock intended, not to awaken the public to current problems, but to use them or go beyond them in revealing man's metaphysical reality, hard as it may be to take. The modern French theatre wants to be metaphysical and such metaphysics can only be brought out through an extreme bewilderment of shocking violence.[20]

It is important to note here that when we speak of the metaphysical interests of the avant-garde theatre, we are in no sense using "metaphysical" to imply a system of coherent concepts regarding man and his world. If these playwrights subscribe to any general notion regarding the nature of the world, it is that the world in which man lives is absurd. But even at the mention of this familiar and popular notion of absurdity we must be careful lest we press quite individual visions of the world into preconceived, philosophical molds. Martin Esslin has been the critic most responsible for popularizing the generic term "theatre of the absurd," taken by many as descriptive of a monolithic avant-garde movement in the theatre. Despite the inadequacies of this term, Esslin is correct when he says,

> The Theatre of the Absurd makes no pretense at explaining the ways of God to man. It can merely present, in anxiety or with derision, an individual human being's intuition of the

ultimate realities as he experiences them; the fruits of one man's descent into the depths of his personality, his dreams, fantasies, and nightmares.

While former attempts at confronting man with the ultimate realities of his condition projected a coherent and generally recognized version of the truth, the Theatre of the Absurd merely communicates one poet's most intimate and personal intuition of the human situation, his own *sense of being*, his individual vision of the world. This is the *subject matter* of the Theatre of the Absurd, and it determines its *form*, which must, of necessity, represent a convention of the stage basically different from the "realistic" theatre of our time.[21]

Esslin's "vision" plus "form" is roughly equivalent to Artaud's "text" plus *"mise en scène,"* Esslin stressing the importance of vision and Artaud stressing *mise en scène.* If we ourselves envision a theatre in which the more traditionally emphasized dialogue and stagecraft are somehow bracketed with poetic vision, on the one side, and with a metaphysically intended *mise en scène,* on the other, we arrive at something approaching the avant-garde theatre. Such a theatre is not new, as Esslin shows in his study of "The Tradition of the Absurd,"[22] but what may be called the angle of vision is new.

As we noted in Chapter 1, the crisis in modern literary criticism centers in the disinclination of critics to deal with the dimensions of the vision informing works of poetic and imaginative significance. Insofar as the avant-garde playwrights intend that their vision will be manifest in the theatre they create, their plays and the vision informing the plays become open to theological criticism. Vision here involves valuations placed upon man, as well as affirmations regarding the nature of ultimate reality. Regardless of the apparent absurdity of the world, affirmations about man are made in terms of what is valued by the playwrights; and in the following chapters we will direct our attention to the theatrical image of this man who is affirmed, in however limited or inverted a fashion. Before doing so, however, we need to make explicit what has been implicit thus far in two assumptions underlying this study.

One assumption is that art expresses genuine insight into the condition and situation of man. "Condition" means whatever is taken as necessary for man's salvation, and salvation ranges all the way from achievement of identity to religious and spiritual fulfillment. "Situation" means man's position in relation to himself and his world. We have seen in Chapter 1 how it is possible to understand human creativity in light of the Christian doctrine of creation. We have also noted the crisis in modern criticism when the vision of the poet is left outside critical considerations. Hence another assumption herein is the relative autonomy of art, i.e., its validity for intuitive cognition alongside other cognitive dimensions of the human spirit, but also its openness both to the greater abundance of life and experience outside literature as well as to theological criticism of its vision and commitments. These two assumptions are well expressed in the celebrated exchange of letters between the late Jean Cocteau and Jacques Maritain entitled *Art and Faith*. Reflecting our first assumption, Maritain says, "In the artist there is a *littérateur*: a double heart, a mummer that would fool God. There is also a craftsman, sometimes a poet: an apprentice of the Creator."[23] And reflecting our second assumption, Cocteau says,

> Literature is impossible. One must get out of it. It is useless to try to get out of it through literature; only love and Faith enable us to get out of ourselves. To resort to dreams is not to leave home; it is searching the attic, where our childhood made contact with poetry.
>
> Art for art's sake, or for the people are equally absurd. I propose art for God.[24]

METHODOLOGICAL QUESTIONS

Having laid the groundwork for a theological critique of the avant-garde French theatre, we must now list the questions which, together with the foregoing assumptions, constitute the methodological approach to the plays we shall analyze. The questions will not be used as a rigid mold into which the plays must be forced. They rather indicate the kinds of questions which come from the groundwork already laid and which provide a means of getting at the images of man presented in the avant-garde theatre.

1. What are the elements of the image of man presented?
   a. Character identity—self-understanding in terms of hopes, fears, expectations, affirmations, memories, regrets, satisfactions, frustrations, etc.
   b. Human relationships which constitute the religious context of love, hate, concern, indifference, etc.
   c. Cosmic relationships which constitute a metaphysical context.
   d. *Mise en scène* insofar as this affects human relationships and cosmic relationships, thus setting limits to what is humanly possible.
   e. Language as a means of communication and as a mode of expressing character identity and human relationships.
   f. Interrelationships of the elements which constitute the form of the image.

2. What assumptions regarding man and his world underlie the choice of the elements of this image of man?
   a. Freedom and necessity.
   b. Individuality and community.
   c. Reason and revelation.
   d. History and existence.
   e. Meaning and non-meaning (absurdity).

3. What does the image assert and affirm about man and his condition and situation?

SAMUEL BECKETT

Among the four playwrights to be considered, Samuel Beckett was the first to gain significant Parisian and then international reputation. With the production of *En Attendant Godot* (*Waiting for Godot*) at the Théâtre de Babylone in January of 1953, the reputations of both Beckett and the avant-garde theatre were established. Despite a 1947 production of Jean Genet's *Les Bonnes* (*The Maids*) and 1950 productions of Arthur Adamov's *L'Invasion* and Eugène Ionesco's *La Cantatrice chauve* (*The Bald Soprano*), it was Beckett's play that catapulted this group of playwrights to wide public notice. These playwrights will be discussed in the order in which they were introduced to American audiences. The plays we will be dealing with all come, essentially, from the decade 1950 to 1960. The major works of Beckett, Ionesco, and Genet have all been translated into English, and references will be made to these texts. Of Adamov's earlier works, with which we will be primarily concerned, the French texts will be used except for *Professor Taranne*.

Two homeless men, a master and his menial, and one boy are the characters of *Waiting for Godot*. The significant images of man in the play center in the two pairs of characters: Vladimir and Estragon, the tramps; and Pozzo and Lucky, the master and menial. A caution is in order here, however: Such descriptive terms as tramp, master, and menial (or slave) are only the most convenient and superficial ways of distinguishing the characters. Beckett is not simply saying that modern man is some sort of tramp on a tramp planet in an endless and purposeless universe. This may be a superficial image supported by the dishabille of the characters' clothes and the barren locale of the stage action, but to move so quickly from immediate visual images to the "meaning" of the play is to judge prematurely what is in reality a very complex presentation of theatrical images. Nor is the judgment warranted that isolates the characters into prototypal identities such as intellectual man (Vladimir), physical man (Estragon, who has even been cast in some productions as a woman), virile tyrant (Pozzo), or impotent slave (Lucky). Each of the characters is vastly more complex than such designations allow, but for purposes of analysis, it is convenient to discuss them as pairs, since Beckett has presented them in this relationship.

As the play opens, Estragon is struggling to get his boot off a rapidly swelling foot. After several fruitless attempts he exclaims, "Nothing to be done."[1] It is a temptation to read the whole play as a kind of homily on this text and to see the characters as no more than minimal men "stripped for inaction."[2] In fact, the characters are faced with two concrete alternatives: waiting for Godot, and suicide. In the course of their wrestling with these alternatives and deciding for the former, we learn and witness the elements of the image of man presented in this couple.

Both Vladimir and Estragon (or Didi and Gogo, as they call each other) spend their days and nights apart and only meet at twilight, the appointed hour for the expected meeting

with Godot. As they attempt to pass the time while waiting,
we learn that Estragon suffers daily beatings from unknown
assailants, that Vladimir suffers from urinary trouble, that
Estragon's feet stink and so does Vladimir's breath, that
Vladimir's hat scratches him and Estragon's boots don't fit;
i.e., that each of them experiences a variety of discomforts and
disabilities which establish them among the world's sufferers.
In response to their situation, Vladimir offers a romantic
vision of suicide, hand in hand from the Eiffel Tower. They
should have done it "a million years ago, in the nineties. . . .
Now it's too late" (p. 7). Now they would not be allowed
to climb the tower. As the dialogue progresses, Estragon
reminds Valdimir that he should button his fly.

VLADIMIR: (*stooping*). True. (*He buttons his fly.*) Never
neglect the little things of life.
ESTRAGON: What do you expect, you always wait till the
last moment.
VLADIMIR: (*musingly*). The last moment . . . (*He medi-
tates.*) Hope deferred maketh the something sick,
who said that? (p. 8)

Estragon is not interested in eschatological speculations, nor
in the book of Proverbs; he wants help with his boot. Vladimir
is reminded of his own problems but while musing on them,
takes off his hat to find the source of the scratch and concludes with "Nothing to be done" (p. 8). The maintenance
of any sustained sequence of thought or action is in fact
impossible. Thus any sustained and orderly account of the
identities of these characters is undercut by the way they are
presented. Nevertheless, some things can be said about the
hopes and fears, the memories and expectations, the dreams
and frustrations which grant a sense of identity to these two
tramps.
   Vladimir and Estragon share the hope that Godot will
come. The expectation is that when Godot does arrive the

enigma of their existence will be resolved. But in trying to remember what they expected to hear from Godot, they become confused.

ESTRAGON: What exactly did we ask him for?
VLADIMIR: Were you not there?
ESTRAGON: I can't have been listening.
VLADIMIR: Oh ... Nothing very definite.
ESTRAGON: A kind of prayer.
VLADIMIR: Precisely.
ESTRAGON: A vague supplication.
VLADIMIR: Exactly (p. 13).

Precision and indefiniteness so intermingle in their memories of encounter with Godot that considerable doubt arises as to whether the encounter ever took place. Vladimir remembers many things quite clearly, whereas Estragon says he either remembers everything or forgets things immediately. The evidence points to the latter, the general forgetfulness of Estragon. In any case, memory is not a dependable index to personal history for these two beings. Dreams, either of the waking or sleeping kind, tend to replace the functions of self-identification more common to modern men.

Vladimir, who appears never to sleep, muses upon such problems as the differences among the Gospels in their accounts of the crucifixion of Jesus and the two thieves. That one thief should be saved he judges a reasonable percentage, but that only one of the four Gospels should refer to this event disturbs him. Estragon, who very readily falls asleep whenever conversation lags or his stomach is temporarily satisfied, dreams violently. He would share his private nightmares, but Valdimir refuses to hear about them. Estragon refuses to enter into Vladimir's speculations about the thieves, instead remembering only the colored maps in a Bible and his dreams of happiness beside the Dead Sea. Thus neither shares concretely in the other's private experience, and the poignancy of this failure at intimacy is underlined by the ironic content of their dreams and memories.

If individual identity is problematic for these tramps, they do have a relationship to each other with some qualitative content. Despite their failure at the level of shared memories and dreams, they realize that they really cannot exist apart from each other. The question of separating is frequently mentioned, but it is always dropped just as suicide is rejected despite the pleasurable contemplation of the sexual overtones of hanging. There is real tenderness in Vladimir's covering the sleeping Estragon with his coat. They frequently embrace in a gesture of genuine affection, even if Estragon is immediately repulsed by Vladimir's reek of garlic. Vladimir seems to be the provident partner to this relationship. He rummages in his pockets for carrots and turnips for Estragon to eat. In return, Estragon "returns the ball" of conversation so that they gain the impression that they exist.

But the very involvement they have with each other raises in Estragon's mind the question of whether they are somehow tied to Godot. Vladimir says, "No question of it. (*Pause.*) For the moment" (p. 14). Do they have to wait? Vladimir has insisted that they will wait until they find out what Godot has to offer, and then they will take it or leave it. But this insistence upon "freedom of the will" is undercut again when the question of taste for carrots leads to the realization that

VLADIMIR: One is what one is.
ESTRAGON: No use wriggling.
VLADIMIR: The essential doesn't change.
ESTRAGON: Nothing to be done (p. 14).

And what is "essential" for these two beings, tied as they are to each other, is the necessity of waiting for Godot.

If a kind of tenderness and affection, as well as genuine fear of loneliness, ties Vladimir and Estragon to each other, it is a literal rope which ties Lucky to Pozzo. The demonic implications of concrete human attachments would seem to be indicated in the relationship between this second couple of beings who appear in both acts of the play. The superficial image of a master and his slave leads to this judgment, but deeper analysis of this couple tends to suspend such an assessment. Since Lucky only speaks when commanded to "think," we are limited to Pozzo's statements regarding the identity of these two beings.

Having announced his name as Pozzo, which draws no recognition from Vladimir and Estragon, Pozzo settles for a more general level of recognition.

> Pozzo: (*halting*). You are human beings none the less. (*He puts on his glasses.*) As far as one can see. (*He takes off his glasses.*) Of the same species as myself. (*He bursts into an enormous laugh.*) Of the same species as Pozzo! Made in God's image! . . .
>
> Yes, gentlemen, I cannot go for long without the society of my likes (*he puts on his glasses and looks at the two likes*) even when the likeness is an imperfect one (pp. 15 f.).

But the likeness between Pozzo and the two tramps stops at the visual similarity. Pozzo's identity really inheres in his relationship to Lucky. How one came to be master and the other menial is a matter of merest chance. Pozzo remarks that their places might just as easily have been reversed "If chance had not willed otherwise. To each one his due" (p. 21). We know nothing of these two apart from what they have offered to each other through the years. Pozzo's life would have been entirely made up of "professional worries" if he had not taken on a "knook" (Lucky). It was Lucky who taught him of "Beauty, grace, truth of the first water" (p. 22). Now that almost sixty years of their relationship have gone by, Pozzo feels himself still young compared with Lucky. But Lucky has the long hair and Pozzo is bald, and thus through sexual symbolism the veracity of Pozzo's self-understanding is put in doubt. Pozzo complains that he now suffers from Lucky's presence and would like to sell him at the fair.

Lucky, who carries a suitcase full of sand, a basket, and a campstool, responds primarily to the imperious commands of Pozzo and to jerks upon the rope encircling his neck. We learn that not only was Lucky at one time a sensitive creature of some esthetic sensibility and philosophical competence, but also he knew a variety of dances. When commanded to dance, he does a sketchy step he calls "the Net." When asked what they would call the dance, Estragon calls it "The Scapegoat's Agony" and Vladimir suggests "The Hard Stool." All three project their own most intimate discomfitures into the interpretations. (A warning, perchance, about our own interpretations of the play!) Lucky's skill seems to have degenerated over the years. When Lucky is called upon to "think," the result is a long, torturous monologue which evokes increasing suffering in Pozzo and finally a wrath of incomprehension in Vladimir and Estragon. Lucky's feelings are really no clearer in their expression. When Pozzo says he is going to sell him, Lucky begins to cry. But Lucky will not accept comfort from Estragon, who receives a sharp kick in the shins for his efforts. Only Pozzo can comfort Lucky. And Lucky will not leave Pozzo. He cannot even be driven away. There is more than the rope tying these two together.

In the second act, when Pozzo and Lucky enter again they are changed characters in that Pozzo is now blind and Lucky is dumb. The rope is now shorter and Pozzo follows more than drives Lucky. But they are still together. They are still on the road. They are not waiting. They are moving, falling down, getting up, struggling from stage left to stage right (which is not quite the same thing as "forward" would suggest) onward to no known end or purpose or direction. Speculation as to why Pozzo and Lucky cannot do without each other is fruitless. They are a couple dependent upon each other for existence, meager though that existence be. The surface relationship of master and slave is thus undercut by a deeper and more complex image of mutual dependence, the tenacity of which is both long-lived and able to withstand physical and spiritual disintegration.

Time is perceived differently by the two couples. Apart from the aforementioned difficulties with memory for Vladimir and Estragon, these two perceive time as that void which must somehow be filled while waiting. Various strategies are pursued to fill the void, all of them essentially linguistic. That is, talking is the means available to fill the void. Apart from a couple of pieces of stage business dealing with carrots and hats, the action is in the waiting. But language provides a variety of possible solutions to the agony of silence and the void. Language also raises the possibility of thought, and thought produces "All the dead voices" talking about "their lives." "To have lived is not enough for them." "They have to talk about it" (p. 40). But for Vladimir and Estragon, talking is also the only means of preventing thought as well as the memory of having thought, which is even more "terrible." What they may have done with their time yesterday is open to question.

VLADIMIR: And where were we yesterday evening according to you?

ESTRAGON: How would I know? In another compartment. There's no lack of void.

VLADIMIR: (*sure of himself*). Good. We weren't here yesterday evening. Now what did we do yesterday evening?

ESTRAGON: Do?

VLADIMIR: Try and remember.

ESTRAGON: Do . . . I suppose we blathered.

VLADIMIR: (*controlling himself*). About what?

ESTRAGON: Oh . . . this and that I suppose, nothing in particular. (*With assurance.*) Yes, now I remember, yesterday evening we spent blathering about nothing in particular. That's been going on now for half a century (p. 42).

It is this "blathering" which fills the void and gives them a sense of existence. When the Boy comes and announces that Godot will not come today but surely tomorrow, the need for talk ends, the night immediately falls and the moon precipitously rises, and the two tramps decide to go away, to act overtly (though they do not move as the curtain descends at the end of both acts).

For Pozzo time is clock time. He will hear none of the suggestion that time has stopped. His watch is an important bit of personal equipment. But somehow he loses or misplaces his watch and immediately panics. He asks Vladimir and Estragon to listen at his vest for the watch ticking somewhere in his clothing. All they can hear is his heart beating a kind of living time. His only response is "Damnation!" (p. 31). In the second act when he is blind, clock time has ceased to have any meaning for him. Vladimir quizzes him on the change that has come over him and Lucky since the day before (or, better, since the first act). In response, Pozzo cries,

> Have you not done tormenting me with your accursed time! It's abominable! When! When! One day, is that not enough for you, one day he went dumb, one day I went blind, one day we'll go deaf, one day we were born, one day we shall die, the same day, the same second, is that not enough for you? (*Calmer.*) They give birth astride of a grave, the light gleams an instant, then it's night once more (p. 57).

The time that had been both cyclical in his watch and linear in his movement becomes merely an instantaneous moment in his blindness, the indefinite moment between birth and death. Questions of when and what take on the negative quality of now dumb, now blind, now deaf, now dead. The question of why is postponed. The question of where takes us into the stage scene itself.

We must not forget that the matters of human identity and human relationship are being presented as stage images, as theatrical images. The *mise en scène*, as we saw in Chapter 2, has implications for both the physical and metaphysical contexts of the images of man presented in the avant-garde theatre. The full significance of the *mise en scène* can be experienced only in an actual production of the plays. However, we can discuss the way in which the playwright envisions the stage scene as a concrete dimension of the total image of man he wishes to present.

In *Waiting for Godot* the place of evening meetings for Vladimir and Estragon is a nearly deserted stage. The only property is a leafless tree. At the back is a cyclorama curtain on which a moon is projected at the end of each act. The lighting is low key. The general feeling engendered by the scene is one of desolation, a gray expanse of uninhabited terrain. For Vladimir and Estragon this is a place of waiting. For Pozzo and Lucky it is a road. For both couples it is also a place of meeting, of encounter, a place for human relationships that is yet no place. Beckett does not allow us to forget that his place of desolation is also a stage in front of which sits an audience. The audience is viewed one moment, through Estragon's eyes, as "Inspiring prospects" (p. 10), and the next moment, through Vladimir's eyes, as "that bog" (p. 10). Just before Pozzo and Lucky enter in the second act, Estragon becomes frightened and tries to run away toward the back wall and becomes entangled in the cyclorama. Vladimir tells him,

. . . Imbecile! There's no way out there. (*He . . . drags him towards front. Gesture towards front.*) There! Not a soul in sight! Off you go! Quick! (*He pushes Estragon towards auditorium. Estragon recoils in horror.*) You won't? (*He contemplates auditorium.*) Well I can understand that (p. 47).

Thus through irony and stage business a Brechtian effect of "alienation" makes the stage both a symbol of the universe and an unmistakably theatrical event compounded of the *mise en scène* elements.

Abundantly clear in this kind of theatre is that the image of man cannot be had in some other way. The presentation in the theatre is as much a part of the image as are any of its elements of language and thought which might be lifted out of the theatrical context and put into some interpretative scheme. But precisely insofar as the image is presented with artistic (i.e., theatrical) integrity, it must be taken seriously as an imaginative prehension of man and his situation.

The human relationships possible between Vladimir and Estragon, Pozzo and Lucky, do not enjoy any of the graciousness of the created world as resource. These relationships are limited and bounded by walls and the ambiguous presence of society (the audience), on the one hand, and, on the other hand, by a natural environment indifferent to man. This is not to credit the natural environment with some sort of mysteriously volitional power in relation to man; it is so to reduce the character of the natural world as to throw man back almost entirely upon himself for any meaning which his life may encompass. We must say "almost" because there is the matter of the few leaves which the tree "grows" between the first and second acts, and the uncertain nightfall and moonrise which seem to depend upon each day's quota of waiting. Not until the Boy comes to announce that Godot will not come does night fall and the moon immediately rise. These events close the two acts in an ironic and amusing way, but also in a way which discloses the inescapable and perhaps meaningless round of the days.

The tree has "enjoyed" a great variety of critical comment. The interpretations include Professor Charles McCoy's conviction that the leaves in the second act testify to God's (Godot's) faithfulness in his appointment in all human relationships. The leaves are the symbol of his already having come. Those who miss the appointment are dead; only the tree (Cross) lives.[3] While this kind of speculation is intriguing, especially to the theologically oriented mind, it seems safer to leave open the question of the precise meaning of the sprouted leaves. But within this openness perhaps we can at least see in the leaves a suggestion of the minimized round of the seasons. Thus the ambiguous and reduced state of the days and seasons further underlines the situation of man thrown back upon himself and his relationships for life's meaning.

Elements of the *mise en scène* we have already noted briefly are the characters' inelegant attire and physical problems. Again the critical commentary on this matter has been rich. For instance, Jean-Jacques Mayoux suggests that the physical grotesqueness and misery of Beckett's characters

> constitute a cruel and humiliating image of man, which echoes that of the nightmare creatures of Bosch and Brueghel; this is a Christian, a Puritan vision of man and his body, and in its bitterness is characteristic of the rebellious Christian.[4]

Whether this is correct or not is less important than the realization that Beckett is presenting characters who have no claim to status in existence, such as clothes might suggest, nor can they escape their bodies into some sort of ascesis. Thus the *mise en scène* as a whole functions primarily to underscore an image of man faced with his metaphysical situation by means of an attenuated and ambiguous physical situation.

When asked about the theme of *Waiting for Godot,* Beckett is reported often to respond by quoting a line from St. Augustine.

> There is a wonderful sentence in Augustine. I wish I could remember the Latin. It is even finer in Latin than in English. "Do not despair: one of the thieves was saved. Do not presume: one of the thieves was damned." . . . I am interested in the shape of ideas even if I do not believe in them. . . . That sentence has a wonderful shape. It is the shape that matters.[5]

Whether the quotation from St. Augustine be the only theme of the play or not (and there is evidence that it is certainly one possible theme) is not so important as the suggestion Beckett gives here about his use of language. By his language he explores the shape of the idea that language does not communicate. Niklaus Gessner, in his study on Beckett, *Die Unzulänglichkeit der Sprache,*[6] has detailed various ways in which language breaks down in the effort of the characters in *Waiting for Godot* to communicate with each other. To use language to communicate the assertion that language does not communicate is either sheer hypocrisy or a monumental artistic tour de force. When asked about this apparent contradiction, Beckett responded to Gessner, *"Que voulez-vous, Monsieur? C'est les mots; on n'a rien d'autre."*[7] If thoughts, beliefs, convictions, assertions, values, memories, feelings, are all doubtful and one is left with only a kind of brute materiality in words, communication is indeed problematic. Beckett tries to show just this situation by his use of language styles drawn from the music hall and circus, patterns of speech in which characters speak past one another. Thus, conceptual thought is rendered highly doubtful in its assertions about meaning in life. Without a language which communicates through commonly held understandings and meanings, no generalized concepts are possible. Thus, we cannot look only to what the characters in *Waiting for Godot* say about themselves and their relationships to locate their identities. Rather, we must hear their language as an element of a total poetic image which includes *mise en scène* as well as gesture and mime.

We have noted how Vladimir and Estragon use language games to fill the void while waiting.[8] It is this game-like character of language which emerges as the fundamental purpose which language has in Beckett's vision. What meanings can be had from language are localized into specific contexts, and the contexts, both personal and situational, are constantly changing. At one point, reflecting Zeno, Estragon remarks, "Everything oozes. It's never the same pus from one second to the next" (p. 39). Thus, despite the seeming stasis of everything in the play, everything yet changes and language is helpless to bridge the chasms between the instants; memory fails; thought breaks down for lack of genuine dialogue. We are left, through a paradoxical situation in which language bombards us with its rich sound and rhythm, with an image in which beings are confronted with each other in their beingness.

We need to be careful lest our own language betray us into conceptualizations which distort the image. Beckett is presenting us with a total, imaginative, poetic, and theatrical image of man which cannot be fairly abstracted from its context in the theatre. That such abstraction, or disengagement, from the theatrical context is necessary for purposes of discussion is unfortunate but not finally disruptive if we keep in mind that there is no real substitute for participation in a performance of the play. But even in reading the play, we can sense the total impact of the image which depends upon the total theatrical event for its significance. It is good to discuss the possible themes and ideas of *Waiting for Godot*, but such discussions pay the price of converting a theatrical image into a conceptual scheme. That price is the living energy of the theatrical image in which the elements of language, gesture, mime, *mise en scène*, presence of the audience—the total theatrical event—evoke and convey an imaginative prehension of existence.

Underlying the image of man as Beckett presents it in *Waiting for Godot* can be discerned some assumptions important for theological assessment of the image. Man is confronted with a situation in which he must wait for significance to meet him. At one point, Estragon asks what has happened to their rights, and Vladimir replies that they gave their rights away. But this happened so long ago, and the event is shrouded in such mystery and doubt, that the situation they face within the context of the play is one in which they do not have freedom, rights. They must wait for Godot. They have only their relationship and an occasional encounter with other men, from which to derive meaning for their lives of waiting. If Godot in any sense symbolizes ultimate significance for their lives, such meaning is indefinitely postponed. The only transcendence possible in their situation is a kind of linguistic transcendence which is really a game to fill the void and help them forget the desperate circumstances of their situation. No meaning comes to them from outside their situations except the necessity of waiting for a meaning that does not come.

There is no general agreement among the critics as to whether these characters are properly taken as individuals or as aspects of a generalized image of man. By discussing the play in terms of its image of man, we are inevitably committed in some sense to the latter, though it is perilous to press such a commitment into any fixed concept of human nature. Beckett's characters are in some identifiable ways individuals, and in other ways symbols of generalized human characteristics. We have seen how Beckett presents couples as the form of human relationship central to his image. It is perhaps pressing the issue too far to assert that what is presented is an image of individuals-in-community. But it can at least be said that the image assumes a relationship between men which is indispensable to any identity which they as individuals might have. There are no dramatic heroes here. There are no clearly defined individuals who face and resolve problems in the ways we are accustomed to look for in Western drama. But it is important to note that regardless of how demonic and destructive the relationship may appear, it is impossible to avoid some form of human engagement with another human in Beckett's image. Loneliness is the great fear in all Beckett's characters. For Vladimir and Estragon loneliness is the most terrible pain they suffer, and it is to be avoided at all costs. It would be far worse for one of them to hang himself successfully and the other be left alive than for them to continue their agonized wait for Godot. Loneliness is unendurable.

We have seen that thought, conceptualization, is highly problematic in any of its presumed deliverances. Vladimir and Estragon continue talking, playing language games, in order not to think. The reasoning faculty is no longer any guarantee of humanity in this image. Vladimir, who comes closest to sustaining any sequence of thought, is always frustrated or diverted from any reasoned conclusions. And just at the point that he comes closest to reasoning through his despair, only to founder in confusion, Godot's messenger, the Boy, arrives to revive hope of Godot's coming while further postponing the event. Neither Vladimir's reasoning nor the disclosures of the messenger resolve the enigma of waiting. We cannot, therefore, assume that Beckett expects answers to the human situation to come from either reason or revelation or any possible combination of the two. If full humanity is dependent upon a high valuation placed upon either reason or revelation, as it does for the humanist and theist respectively, then no full humanity is forthcoming from Beckett's image. On the other hand, precisely because the deliverances of both reason and revelation are rendered problematic by the exigencies of modern existence, Beckett's image of man waiting and filling his time with what tenderness and joy can be mustered claims some attention as a serious envisagement of life's possibilities.

The few references in *Waiting for Godot* to events in the past, vague memories, mysterious evocations of the passage of time do not conspire to suggest anything approaching a sense of historical existence. Heidegger's *geworfenheit* (thrown into existence) is far more descriptive of the situation for Vladimir and Estragon, as well as for Pozzo and Lucky, than is any assumption which would try to see purpose or even development in their existence. Each day is the same and concludes with waiting for Godot. This does not mean that Beckett works within an existentialist framework similar to Sartre's, for instance. Beckett is concerned with existence and makes existential assumptions, but he is not existentialist in any formal and philosophical sense. His focus is upon existence in its bare necessities. He is not concerned with history, only with the existential situation in which man is faced with himself and his world.

The precise nature of man's world is problematic, as we have seen. On the basis of the evidence in *Waiting for Godot*, we would have to say that man is not at home in his world. This is not to suggest that he can, or even tries very hard to, escape from his world, including his body. It is to suggest that for Beckett the world does not in any simple way embody meaning which man can discern and come to terms with. An open question is whether Beckett assumes that man does not possess the equipment to wrestle meaning from his world or whether the world is frankly enigmatic, at the most, and strictly non-meaningful, at the least. Nothing about the world is assured. Pozzo can wax lyrical about how nightfall is "charging" and will soon "pop" upon the scene, but in the next moment we discover that it is merely Pozzo's romantic bubble which pops in a petering out of his verbal excitement. The whole enterprise was merely verbal and had no reference to any real world. When night does come, it comes as a surprise if also as a relief because it ends the day's quota of waiting. In Beckett's vision man is faced less with a world than with the threat of nonexistence. It is not that the world threatens to crush man, but that man can draw no assured sense from his physical environment that he in fact possesses a metaphysical environment.

In the image of man as Beckett presents it in *Waiting for Godot*, man is a being in relationship. The quality of this relationship turns upon how individual men-in-relationship respond to the situation in which they find themselves. This is essentially Kenneth Rexroth's point when he says,

> If we refuse to accept the world on secular terms, Godot isn't coming. If we accept it for ourselves, the comradeship of men, whether verminous tramps with unmanageable pants or Jim and Huck Finn drifting through all the universe on their raft—the comradeship of men in work, in art, or simply in waiting, in the utterly unacquisitive act of waiting—is an ultimate value, so ultimate that it gives life sufficient dignity and satisfaction. So say Homer and Samuel Beckett and everybody else, too, who has ever been worth his salt.[9]

But Rexroth fails to grasp that in Beckett's vision Godot does not come, whether Vladimir and Estragon wait with acceptance or impatience. They find a kind of comradeship while waiting, but this is a gesture of desperation since they must wait. The comradeship is never fully satisfying in itself. To be sure, what dignity there is for man in Beckett's vision centers in his faithfulness to his comrade. But there is always doubt about this because of the necessity of waiting together. Man is not really free either to commit himself to relationships or to withdraw from them. Relationships are a part of man's situation, and there are no absolute guidelines for how relationships will be pursued. They can be demonic, as with Pozzo and Lucky, as well as compassionate, as with Vladimir and Estragon. Beckett would appear to put some weight in favor of the latter, but we must remember we are dealing with an image presented in the theatre, and thus the question is always open as to the playwright's own ultimate convictions.

In Beckett's image of man, the possibilities for creative activity are almost entirely linguistic and mimetic. These are the activities which fill the time-void for Vladimir and Estragon and give them a sense of existence. Any ultimate significance attributable to these few possibilities is seriously doubted in Vladimir's long speech near the end of the second act, just before the Boy enters:

> Was I sleeping, while the others suffered? Am I sleeping now? To-morrow, when I wake, or think I do, what shall I say of to-day? That with Estragon my friend, at this place, until the fall of night, I waited for Godot? That Pozzo passed, with his carrier, and that he spoke to us? Probably. But in all that what truth will there be?
> (*Estragon, having struggled with his boots in vain, is dozing off again. Vladimir looks at him.*) He'll know nothing. He'll tell me about the blows he received and I'll give him a carrot. (*Pause.*) Astride of a grave and a difficult birth. Down in the hole, lingeringly, the grave-digger puts on the forceps. We have time to grow old. The air is full of our cries. (*He listens.*) But habit is a great deadener. (*He looks again at Estragon.*) At me too someone is looking, of me too someone is saying, He is sleeping, he knows nothing, let him sleep on. (*Pause.*) I can't go on! (*Pause.*) What have I said? (p. 58)

Who is looking at Vladimir? Certainly the audience is looking at him. Is this a reference to a transcendent being? That is and remains a question. While the significance of what he has said is open to doubt, that he has said something, that he has acted, that through language and gesture time is filled— these things are relatively assured. There is here no *cogito, ergo sum*; there is at best an assertion that so long as language and action continue, there are possibilities for compassionate human relationships. In this situation Vladimir's theatrical gesture of placing his coat over the sleeping Estragon is as close as Beckett's man can come to an ultimate gesture. But the final irony is the possibility that even this gesture may take place only in a dream.

EUGÈNE IONESCO

If we may speak of the four avant-garde playwrights we are considering as a group, Eugène Ionesco is in many ways the most "available." He has written widely concerning his own work. He has "enjoyed" a lengthy newspaper debate with British critics, notably Kenneth Tynan. His influence is seen quite readily in the work of Harold Pinter in Britain and Edward Albee in the United States. The sheer magnitude of his dramatic output, while composed mostly of shorter pieces, has meant that he has been fairly continuously before the public eye since the early 1950's. The plenitude of his works, no one of which has the stature of *Waiting for Godot*, makes analysis of his vision of man difficult. Any selection taken as representative of his whole work is necessarily arbitrary but cannot be avoided. Keeping in mind this situation we will discuss *The Lesson*, a shorter, early play, and *Victims of Duty*, a longer, later play.

Before we turn to the plays, however, a few comments are in order regarding Ionesco's extensive commentary on his own work, since much of his "availability" inheres in these articles. Ionesco has been at some pains to articulate his own "point of departure" in the theatre, as well as his relationship to the avant-garde movement and to what he considers to be his own "classicism."[1]

The point has often been made that the avant-garde playwrights are interested in projecting upon the stage highly individual and personal visions of what it means to be alive, to exist. While this generalization pertains in some sense to the four men we are discussing, Ionesco expresses this judgment, in relation to himself, in a particular way. In his well-known essay, "The Point of Departure," he says,

> But since the microcosm is in the image of the macrocosm, and each of us is all others, it is in the deepest parts of myself, my anguish, my dreams, it is in my solitude that I have the greatest chance of finding that which is universal.[2]

This is more than an existentialist statement. Ionesco is convinced that the elements of his own interior solitude are shared by all men and that he will be truest to the common condition of all men precisely by projecting upon the stage his own interior vision. This is not the same thing as asserting that there is something called human nature which sets men off from other beings and relates them to a transcendent source of meaning and existence. That assertion, in Ionesco's eyes, is a matter of ideology, of doctrine, and this he wants to avoid. But his understanding of the imagistic relationship between his own inner vision and the interior condition of all men does allow us to see his plays as intentional images of man. The question is, What man?

The world in which Ionesco finds his own existence is an unstable world, a world of extremes.

> ... [the] anguish [resulting from a sense of disorientation] is suddenly transformed into liberty; nothing is important any longer but the wonder of being, the new and surprising consciousness of our existence in a light of dawn, and in a new-found freedom; we are astounded to discover that we exist in this world that appears illusory, fictitious—where human behavior reveals its absurdity, and all history, its absolute use-

lessness; all reality, all language seems to become disjointed, to fall apart, to empty itself of meaning, so that, since all is devoid of importance, what else can one do but laugh at it?[3]

Within this experience of the instability of the world and the "laughability" of human behavior, Ionesco finds reflected the two moods underlying his plays.

> Two fundamental states of consciousness are at the root of all my plays. Sometimes one dominates, sometimes the other; sometimes they are mingled. These two basic feelings are those of evanescence on the one hand, and heaviness on the other; of emptiness and of an overabundance of presence; of the unreal transparency of the world, and of its opaqueness; of light, and of heavy shadows.[4]

It is, however, the mood of darkness and heaviness which dominates Ionesco's consciousness; consequently this mood dominates his plays, particularly the early ones. Ionesco describes the feeling when he says,

> A curtain, an insuperable wall, comes between me and the world, between me and myself; matter fills everything, taking up all space, annihilates all liberty under its weight; the horizon shrinks, and the world becomes a stifling dungeon. Speech crumbles, but in another way, words fall like stones, like corpses; I feel myself overcome by heavy forces against which I wage a losing battle.[5]

In such a world only humor, even the kind of hopeless humor elicited by the absurdity of human action, has about it the quality of "salvation."[6]

Ionesco's concept of the avant-garde theatre is related to his microcosm-macrocosm image for his own theatrical works. The true avant-garde is not invention, but a return to what is truly theatrical, the intolerable situation of man.[7] He is fond of referring to the prison of Shakespeare's *Richard II* as a type of the prison of existence in which all men are caught. By cutting through what he considers to be the hidebound "traditionalism" of the theatre, he hopes to show "that all truth and all reality is classical and eternal."[8] As he says,

> What people call the avant-garde is interesting only if it marks a return to the sources, only if it joins a living tradition, across a sclerosed traditionalism, across worn-out academicism. . . . The youngest and newest works of art are recognizable, and speak to all ages. Yes, it is King Solomon who is my true leader, and Job—Beckett's contemporary.[9]

As early as 1953, Ionesco had written:

> For me, the theatre—mime—is most often a confession: I only make avowals (incomprehensible to the deaf, but that can't be helped), for what else can I do? I try to project upon the stage an inner drama (incomprehensible to myself) telling myself, nevertheless, that since the microcosm is an image of the macrocosm, it may happen that this torn up, disarticulated inner world is in some way the mirror or symbol of universal contradictions.[10]

He identifies this personal vision with the true avant-garde, for it is precisely the contents of his own inner vision that he finds in what he calls the "classical" tradition. In 1961 he wrote:

> And what remains that is fundamental or permanent in these new works, among the ruins of systems of thought *of all kinds* (and not only those of such or such a society)? Mockery, anguish, a pure state of confusion, fear; that is to say, the essentially human, tragic, reality, which from time to time, a doctrine or a faith succeeds in covering.[11]

And thus we see that he claims Job and King Solomon as spiritual ancestors, not because they are religious figures in any sense, but because they and Richard II share in the anguish, confusion, and fear that he finds dominant in his own interior vision of existence. And his concern is to produce a theatre which expresses this "essential" humanity.

In *The Lesson*[12] there are three characters: the Professor, the Pupil, and the Maid. The primary image of the human situation is revealed in the relationship between the Professor and the Pupil. As the play begins, the girl student arrives for her first lesson with the Professor. These characters have no names, only functional designations. We learn that the Pupil has come to prepare for her "total doctorate." She is vivacious and confident. She tells us that her parents are wealthy and want to help her in her studies. She has accepted from them the belief that a "little general culture, even if it is solid, is no longer enough, in these times" (p. 49). She already has earned high school diplomas in science and arts, and with this background she is confident that in three weeks she can, with the Professor's help, prepare herself for her doctoral examinations. Beyond these few hints of her background, her educational aspirations, her acceptance of her parents' views, we know nothing of her identity. But we do see her change as a person in the course of her relationship to the Professor.

We learn from the Professor that he has lived in his (unnamed) town for thirty years, but that he would just as soon live in Bordeaux or Paris, though he has never visited either. He is a timid man, very polite and very much the Professor. At one point he recalls an acquaintance he knew during his military days, long ago. Other than these few hints we learn nothing about his identity as a person.

Both the Professor and the Pupil share in the general bourgeois situation. The few suggestions as to their backgrounds are not meant really to identify them beyond this general way, and the language they use to tell us what little we learn of them is the clichè language of the middle class. They are less persons than they are types.

In commenting on his first play, *The Bald Soprano*,[13] Ionesco has said:

The Smiths, the Martins, can no longer talk because they can no longer think; they can no longer think *because they can no longer be moved, can no longer feel passions*; they can no longer be, they can "become" anybody, anything, for, having lost their identity, they assume the identity of others, become part of the world of the impersonal; they are interchangeable: you can put Martin in place of Smith and vice versa, no one will notice.[14]

While it is not clear that either the Professor or the Pupil ever had an identity to lose, it does become evident that they can "become" someone or something else in their relationship to each other. To achieve this change in character, Ionesco uses essentially linguistic means. That is to say, between these two characters there is primarily a linguistic relationship in which the traditional substantive nature of human character is replaced by the substantive nature of language.

The Professor begins by asking simple questions of geography and arithmetic. We discover that the Pupil can only add, she cannot subtract, and multiplication is difficult. In learning these limitations of the Pupil's knowledge and ability, we also learn that it is difficult for the Professor to communicate with the Pupil. Their dialogue assumes much the form of a dance which ends, with each subject matter, in an impasse. Each time this occurs, tension is increased in the relationship between the two. The arithmetic lesson ends on the matter of multiplication. The Professor asks an impossible question:

PROFESSOR: . . . how much, for example, are three billion seven hundred fifty-five million nine hundred ninety-eight thousand two hundred fifty-one, multiplied by five billion one hundred sixty-two million three hundred and three thousand five hundred and eight:

PUPIL: (*very quickly*). That makes nineteen quintillion three hundred ninety quadrillion two trillion eight hundred forty-four billion two hundred nineteen million one hundred sixty-four thousand five hundred and eight. . . .

PROFESSOR: . . . But how did you know that, if you don't know the principles of arithmetical reasoning?

PUPIL: It's easy. Not being able to rely on my reasoning, I've memorized all the products of all possible multiplications (pp. 58 f.).

The Professor is not at all happy with the Pupil's way of going about achieving her answers, for she does not really "understand" what she is doing. He concludes the impasse in understanding with the assertion,

. . . It is by mathematical reasoning, simultaneously inductive and deductive, that you ought to arrive at this result—as well as at any other result. Mathematics is the sworn enemy of memory, which is excellent otherwise, but disastrous, arithmetically speaking! . . . (p. 59)

Memory and reasoning are clearly at cross purposes here. Memory provides no useful clues to personal identity, only useless information. Reasoning does not solve problems; it has only the quality of a hostile gesture in the words of the Professor. Thus, both mental processes, memory and reasoning, provide not communication and understanding but impasse and tension in the relationship between these two characters. The result is a decreased vitality on the part of the Pupil and an increased nervousness on the part of the Professor.

Just as the Professor suggests that they move on to another subject, philology, the Maid enters and warns the Professor to take it easy. She tells him that "philology leads to calamity." The Professor brushes aside her warning and plunges into a discussion of the "neo-Spanish" languages. We learn that one is able to distinguish the several languages in this group (Spanish, Latin, Italian, French, Portuguese, Roumanian, Sardinian or Sardanapalian, and neo-Spanish, the mother tongue of which is "Spanishe, with a mute *e*")

> thanks to their distinctive characteristics, absolutely indis-
> putable proofs of their extraordinary resemblance, which
> renders indisputable their common origin, and which, at the
> same time differentiates them profoundly—through continu-
> ation of the distinctive traits which I've just cited (p. 61).

It comes as no surprise that the Pupil cannot in fact pronounce
correctly any given term in any of these several "languages."
On the one hand,

> . . . for the word "Italy," in French we have the word
> "France," which is an exact translation of it. My country is
> France. And "France" in Oriental: "Orient!" My country is
> the Orient. And "Orient" in Portuguese: "Portugal!" . . . And
> so on . . . (p. 69)

While on the other hand,

> . . . when a Spaniard says: "I reside in the capital," the word
> "capital" does not mean at all the same thing that a Portuguese
> means when he says: "I reside in the capital." All the more so
> in the case of a Frenchman, a neo-Spaniard, a Roumanian,
> a Latin, a Sardanapali . . . (p. 70)

All words are the same and all words are different. As the
Professor tries ever harder to get this information across
to the Pupil, he becomes increasingly excited. Her response is
to develop a toothache. Increasingly, her total attention is
turned in upon her pain, and at the same time, her reactions
become slower and slower.

We learn from the Professor's discourse that words do
not have the kind of referential meaning they normally are
taken to have. Instead, they become objects in themselves.
In trying to teach the Pupil how to pronounce correctly,
the Professor describes how words

> . . . become filled with warm air that is lighter than the sur-
> rounding air so that they can fly without danger of falling on
> deaf ears, which are veritable voids, tombs of sonorities. If
> you utter several sounds at an accelerated speed, they will
> automatically cling to each other, constituting thus syllables,
> words, even sentences, that is to say groupings of various

importance, purely irrational assemblages of sounds, denuded of all sense, but for that very reason the more capable of maintaining themselves without danger at a high altitude in the air. By themselves, words charged with significance will fall, weighted down by their meaning, and in the end they always collapse, fall . . . (pp. 62 f.)

As their conversation progresses, the Professor's words more and more fall on the Pupil's deaf ears, and in time his words become blunt instruments with which he attacks her.

The scene of *The Lesson* is laid in a provincial drawing room of rather meager proportions and appointments. Ionesco seems to favor the imaginative use of invisible objects, as though to underscore the substantive nature of the language he uses to describe them. This is notably true of the invisible "knife" which the Professor brandishes in the closing moments of the play. We have noted how the kind of language games played by the Professor and his Pupil take on a dance form. In the final scene, when the Professor is trying to instruct the Pupil in how to pronounce the word "knife" in the several neo-Spanish tongues, Ionesco calls for his circling about her in a kind of "scalp dance," though this is only to be suggested. The climax of this action is the mimed rape-murder of the Pupil, thus concluding at last the frustrated dances of language previously attempted. In this way the *mise en scène* intensifies and supports the role of language more than it does the characterizations of the principle players.

As has become evident in this discussion, it is impossible to say anything about Ionesco's theatre without treating his use of language. It is important to note that what often appears to be a didactic use of language is not really so in *The Lesson.* The Professor reiterates the importance of understanding, of communication, between himself and the Pupil. He extols the simple virtue of practice, of experience, in the use and pronunciation of various languages only to vitiate his "teaching" by saying, "It's a matter of having a certain experience . . . in these diverse languages, which are so diverse in spite of the fact that they present wholly identical characteristics" (p. 68). When speaking of the root meanings of terms, the Professor is asked, "Are the roots of words square?" He answers, "Square or cube. That depends" (p. 65). In this situation, where even the rules of grammar are turned in upon themselves and confused with arithmetical rules, it becomes difficult to accept any statement at its face value. Didacticism, in its normal forms, is quite out of the question. By his skillful use of language, Ionesco manages to distort language into a substantive form which becomes a tool of aggression in the hands of the Professor.

The final act of violence, the symbolic rape-murder by a "knife" which is only a word, is prepared for in the Professor's earlier discussion of how words are formed. Meaningless words, filled with warm air, float upon the breezes and cause no problem. But words with meanings attached fall and break. Immediately following this disclosure of a language "theory," the Pupil develops her toothache. Increasingly, as the words tumble out of the Professor's mouth, the Pupil's mouth hurts more and more, and her ears become deafer and deafer to his words. The irony here is that the Professor's words are neither the totally senseless words that keep from falling on deaf ears nor the words charged with meaning which fall of their own dead weight. We find ourselves in a situation in which it seems that the Professor's theory of language should provide for a middle case, in which meaningless (or nearly meaningless) words stop up the ears of the listener, thus frustrating communication in the very act of attempting it. That the Professor's words take on this kind of substantive quality seems evident in the light of the rape-murder. The only communication possible here is like that of the torture machine in Kafka's *The Penal*

Colony. The machine, with its etching needles, writes the crime of the prisoner into his back, deeper and deeper until he "understands." Of course, he dies in the moment of "truth." The same is true for the Pupil. She dies at the moment she "understands" that the knife kills, as the Professor has been telling her.

In *The Lesson* we are confronted not so much with an image of man as with an image of human mental and spiritual attributes which have become autonomous. Notably reason and language are the primary elements of the image in this play, as reflected in arithmetic and philology. But these elements of human existence are presented in such a way that they take on autonomous existences of their own and use men for their own irrational ends. J. S. Doubrovsky comments that Ionesco's use of language

> ... is a perpetually renewed act of accusation against language, a language that lends itself to all possible coaxings and inveiglements, torsions and distortions, that can utter contrary statements in one breath and believes itself to be an emanation of the universal Logos! Instead of men using language to think, we have language thinking for men.[15]

In *The Lesson*, both language and mathematics become the users of men. It is as though these two most prized elements of "human nature" (at least to the modern, non-Christian mind) have disengaged themselves from their human sources and have joined in an unholy alliance against man. The image is that of man tryannized by his own mental and spiritual powers. The treacherous situation for man faced with autonomous language and reason is summed up by the Maid when she says, "Arithmetic leads to philology, and philology leads to crime" (p. 76).

In *Victims of Duty*[16] Ionesco makes explicit in several ways what he feels to be the victimized state of man. Professor

Leonard C. Pronko feels that this play does not come off as drama, that it is well subtitled as a "pseudo-drama," and that it is too obscure in its dramatic action. He also classifies this play as another (together with *The Lesson* and others) example of Ionesco's preoccupation with totalitarianism.[17] While all these judgments are correct, at least on one level, they do not obviate the importance of *Victims of Duty* precisely because the many elements of this play, leading to the obscurity of which Pronko speaks, illuminate Ionesco's image of man.

The man-woman relationship, particularly the marriage relationship (e.g., *The Bald Soprano, The Chairs*,[18] *Amédée*,[19] etc.), is important in Ionesco's image of man. In *Victims of Duty* we see a typical petty bourgeois, childless couple spending the evening in a conventional and apparently habitual fashion; she (Madeleine) is darning socks, and he (Choubert) is reading the newspaper. Out of this prosaic situation emerges a fantastic theatrical presentation that hinges on the question of human identity. And the theatrical event is given double significance by Ionesco because the question of identity is inextricably bound up with a theory of theatre in the dialogue of the play.

We learn nothing of Madeleine's background. Of her hopes, fears, expectations, affirmations, memories, etc., we know almost nothing. At one point she wishes she had had a girl child, but this tells us little. She is well adjusted to her society. She tells us that

> . . . the law *is* necessary, and what's necessary and indispensable is *good*, and everything that's good is *nice*. And it really is very nice indeed to be a good, law-abiding citizen and do one's duty and have a clear conscience! . . . (p. 118)

Whether she or anyone else is in fact able to achieve this bourgeois ideal never enters her head. She mouths the platitudes she finds "necessary" and "nice" in her society, thus comfortably conforming to its expectations. In her world, there is really "nothing new under the sun. Even when there isn't any" (p. 119). Madeleine is an example of the kind of character who can "become" anyone, and Ionesco uses her in just this way as she successively "becomes" a temptress, an old woman, Choubert's mother, a theatregoer; and in between she is sometimes the Detective's mistress as well as Choubert's wife. In all these "roles" Madeleine is, or becomes, a reflection of what others require in the pursuit of their interests and concerns. She has no real center to herself. Even in relation to Choubert, she is most often a kind of interlocutor who merely provides him with the questions that allow him to articulate his theories on government and the theatre. And at the end of the play, she becomes the instrument of one of Ionesco's favorite preoccupations, the material abundance and oppressiveness of the universe. When asked to prepare some coffee, she keeps bringing in cups until the sideboard is completely covered. Her actions become automatic as she moves from kitchen to parlor, bringing more and more cups. She is indeed victimized by what she feels to be her duty both to others and to her world.

We are introduced to Choubert as a man who worries over the tendency of government suggestions to become fixed rules. For unknown reasons the government of his country is recommending that citizens "cultivate detachment" (p. 118). When reminded of the value of the law by his wife, Choubert rationalizes his frustrated liberality with the thought, "Renunciation has one important advantage: it's political and mystical at the same time. It bears fruit on two levels" (p. 118). This banal approach to politics is followed by his ideas on the theatre. He fancies himself something of a student of the drama:

> All the plays that have ever been written, from Ancient Greece to the present day, have never really been anything but thrillers. Drama's always been realistic and there's always been a detective about. Every play's an investigation brought

to a successful conclusion. There's a riddle, and it's solved in the final scene. Sometimes earlier. You seek, and then you find. Might as well give the game away at the start (p. 119).

Choubert lumps the French classical theatre, the Miracle Plays (where, he says, we ought to forget about the divine intervention business anyway), and the naturalistic theatre of Antoine into this same classification. We are tempted to take his words as the theories of Ionesco when suddenly Choubert considers Madeleine's suggestion of checking his theories with the acknowledged critics. She offers,

> Oh, there's bound to be someone, among the cinema enthusiasts, or the professors at the *Collège de France*, the influential members of the Agricultural School, the Norwegians or some of those veterinary surgeons . . . A vet, now there's someone who should have lots of ideas (p. 120).

Even the tradition of Ibsen has scant chance of getting a fair hearing when thrown together with professors of agronomy and with veterinary surgeons as drama theorists. But Choubert's theories are put immediately to the test with the entrance of the Detective upon the scene.

The Detective (who calls himself Chief Inspector) has come to the house looking for the concierge in order to ask the whereabouts of the former occupants of Choubert's apartment. The concierge being out, he knocks on Choubert's door, and is asked in, since he is such a "nice young man." Soon he asks Choubert whether he knew the former tenant and whether the name was "Mallot" with a "t" or "Mallod" with a "d." Choubert immediately and unhesitatingly answers, "Mallot" with a "t." With this bit of information established, the Detective makes himself at home and begins to interrogate Choubert further on his knowledge of the Mallots. But Choubert is immediately thrown into what might be called a seizure of epistemological doubt.

DETECTIVE: So you knew the Mallots?
CHOUBERT: [*somewhat intrigued*] No. I never knew them.
DETECTIVE: Then how do you know their name ends in a t?
CHOUBERT: [*very surprised*] Why yes, of course, you're
          right . . . How *do* I know? *How* do I know?
          . . . How do I *know*? . . . I don't know how I
          know! (p. 124)

As the interrogation proceeds, Choubert becomes suddenly
very tired, much like the Pupil developed her toothache in
The Lesson. He can't remember where he must have known
or even met Mallot. Possible places were those we all customarily associate with contexts for former friendships: the
house we lived in as a child, school, the army, a friend's
house, or even our own wedding. None of these contexts suf-
fices in memory for the identification of Mallot. Consequently, the Detective forces Choubert to begin probing his
unconscious memory in search of Mallot. In this way, Ionesco
seems to be saying that this play, this bourgeois, naturalistic,
"thriller," is to be identified with the modern tradition of
psychological drama deriving from Ibsen. But we must be
careful not to make premature judgments here. We are looking for Mallot!

It soon becomes abundantly clear that the search for Mallot is really a search for Choubert's own identity. Choubert
first goes "down" beyond the "sound barrier" and even beyond the "sight barrier" right past his relationship with Madeleine. That relationship is depicted with her as temptress and
then as an old woman, while Choubert prattles the banal
phrases of the lover. When he finally emerges from the depths,
he is transformed into himself as a child. Madeleine becomes
his mother, who died early, and the Detective becomes his
father, with whom he could not communicate. In subsequent
scenes the search is pursued up imaginary mountains and in
flight from their tops. On the "misty flats" between the depths

and heights the search is conducted as a play within the play. The Detective and Madeleine become the spectators and Choubert a monologist. His words disclose the painful-joyful inner world of dream and hallucination, with images of the "yawning pit" and "hopeless hope." Madeleine complains that he only contradicts himself and that the "play" could have been more amusing or at least instructive. Choubert is finally "brought back to earth" from these pseudo-psychoanalytical searchings, but without having found Mallot.

The Detective's solution to Choubert's failure is to force Choubert to eat great crusts of bread to "plug up the gaps" in his memory. Pursuing the "thriller" motif, Choubert is temporarily saved from more stuffing by the unexpected arrival of his friend, Nicolas d'Eu. In melodramatic fashion, Nicolas murders the by-now demonic Detective, whose last words are "Long live the white race!" and "I am . . . a victim . . . of duty!" (p. 165). But Nicolas in turn succumbs to duty and takes the Detective's place as Choubert's torturer, forcing him to chew and swallow yet more great crusts of bread. Mallot is never found.

In this enigmatic and inconclusive termination to the search for Mallot-Choubert, we are not sure whether Ionesco has used the identity question as a pretext for enunciating theories of the theatre in order to destroy them by irony and humor or whether his concern for man is inextricably bound up with his notion of the theatre as a place where an image is to be presented.[20] The evidence seems to favor the latter, especially when we learn from Nicolas d'Eu his ideas for a new theatre. Reflecting Ionesco's early essay, "No," in which the effort was made to assert the identity of opposites, Nicolas says,

> . . . I should introduce contradiction where there is no con-
> tradiction, and no contradiction where there is what com-
> mon-sense usually calls contradiction . . . We'll get rid of the
> principle of identity and unity of character and let movement

and dynamic psychology take its place . . . We are not ourselves . . . Personality doesn't exist.

. . .

The characters lose their form in the formlessness of becoming. Each character is not so much himself as another.

. . .

As for plot and motivation, let's not mention them. . . . No
more drama, no more tragedy: the tragic's turning comic, the
comic is tragic, and life's getting more cheerful . . . more
cheerful . . . (pp. 158 f.)

These ideas are in direct opposition to those of the Detective,
who describes himself as

. . . Aristotelically logical, true to myself, faithful to my duty
and full of respect for my bosses . . . I don't believe in the
absurd, everything hangs together, everything can be com-
prehended in time . . . thanks to the achievements of human
thought and science (p. 159).

We have noted how Choubert has described the "Aristotelically logical" play as no more than a thriller and how Ionesco's own commentary on his work seems to support Nicolas' notions for a new theatre. But our desire to read into
Nicolas' speech a direct expression of Ionesco's own theatrical
intentions, as well as his psychology, is undercut when Nicolas himself becomes a victim of duty and forces poor Choubert
to eat more bread. We must separate the image from the
ideology.

Despite the tendency for ideology to become tyrannical,
the image of man presented in *Victims of Duty* is in keeping
with the notions of Nicolas insofar as they point to an imaginative theatrical image. Any possible form for Madeleine is lost in
continually becoming others. As Choubert "becomes" other
manifestations of himself in quasi-Freudian fashion, we discover that the process has no end. None of the relationships
customarily thought to bring substance and quality to personal identity achieves any significant end for Choubert. His

relationship with his mother is shown to founder on the impossibility of learning or expressing forgiveness. His relationship with his father is frustrated by absolute incommunicability between them. He never knows Madeleine as more than a projection of his own lusts or sense of guilt at her growing old. It is questionable whether he exists as an individual at all, except as a theatrical image of a man searching for identity. At one point he petulantly tells the Detective that Mallot has other names, too: "Marius, Marin, Lougastec, Perpignan, Manchecroche . . . His last name was Machecroche!" (p. 154). With such a progression of mysterious names, Mallot-Choubert fares well to become Everyman, or perhaps it is a case of his really being no one. The difference is, of course, great, but it rests with interpretation of the play and not with the image Ionesco presents, which seems to be consciously enigmatic.

Choubert is related to the cosmos only in terms of a certain interest in matters of time and in terms of a universe overabundantly supplied with matter. Neither of these concerns is worked out with any great detail. A couple of references to the Detective's gold watch and the great crusts of bread suffice to suggest a kind of uncertainty about time and a painful awareness of abundant matter. The abundance of coffee cups which Madeleine brings in help point toward a "heavy" universe as man's "home." But none of these matters helps establish any identity for Choubert. At most, they suggest that his world offers him little helpful support in his search for identity.

The *mise en scène* is full of theatrical tricks: blackouts, a play within the play, climbing under tables to "go down" and onto tables and chairs to project upon the stage the inner climb up a mountain of memories, recorded voices—all against the background of a bourgeois living room. Because of the diverse, perhaps uncontrolled, wealth of theatricalism in the play, the *mise en scène* fails to give more than a sense of near chaos as the metaphysical environment in which Choubert must search for Mallot. Nevertheless, we are not allowed to forget that we are witnessing a theatrical presentation. This is Ionesco's presentation of an inner perception of the problem which man faces when he tries to make sense of his existence in a world of chaos, both internal and external.

In an essay on Ionesco's language, Jean Vannier discusses the way in which Ionesco, together with Samuel Beckett and Arthur Adamov, creates "a dramaturgy of human relations at the level of language itself."[21] Vannier's thesis is that all of Ionesco's theatre opens onto a "night of silence." Within the immense vitality and variety of Ionesco's language, Vannier finds the silence of a universe which finally closes upon the *"absense* of humanity."[22] At the close of *Victims of Duty* language is joined with the crust of bread to further brutalize the helpless Choubert. We saw a similar "linguistic" event at the close of *The Lesson,* where a verbal knife became an instrument of violence, and the only mutually supportive and "communicative" expression shared by the Pupil and the Professor was her dying gasp and his gasp of psycho-sexual release. In Choubert's case his own expressive possibilities are completely voided by the words filling his ears and the bread filling his mouth. The result is silence for Choubert, both in his hearing and in his speaking. We are terrified by the vision of several characters joined in chanting "Chew! Swallow! Chew! Swallow!" (p. 166) as they pass the bread to one another in a kind of inverted sacrament. The duty imposed upon Choubert becomes the duty mutually imposed upon all, for these men indeed live by bread alone. There is no spirit in a world where words lead to tyranny and silence and no redeeming Word can be heard. But this is the theatre.

Ionesco has said in his essay, "Theatre and Anti-Theatre,"

I conceive of a pure theatre. To achieve it, destroy the usual, coherent, rational language; make of the text a pretext for a play; liberate actors and spectators from the mania of intentional messages and other constraints, from their solitude, from themselves. A theatrical work has no *conscious* intention to teach you anything at all; it causes you to reflect, that is in spite of itself, and outside itself. It should tend only to liberate.[23]

We can see the influence of Artaud in this statement; we can read Ionesco's plays in the light of it, and it suggests that we must beware lest our "reflections" impute a teaching to Ionesco which he does not himself admit. But insofar as he has consciously intended to project upon the stage an image of his own inner, microcosmic vision, we can at least try to identify the elements of this image: elements of identity (or lack of it), relationships granting meaning to existence (or lack of them), cosmic relationships, *mise en scène* as an imaginative context for the image, and language. And because Ionesco is serious both about man and about the theatre, we can attempt to elucidate the assumptions underlying the choice of elements in his image of man.

In both *The Lesson* and *Victims of Duty* man is shown to make a brave attempt at freedom of thought and independence of action, only to be quickly suppressed by tyrannous forces. The Pupil is quickly subdued by the Professor, whose theories of language become ideological instruments of torture. Choubert is quickly forced into a humiliating sequence of actions by the Detective's pseudo-psychological determination to achieve answers to his questions. In both cases man is victimized by something: language, ideology, duty, the material world. Man is not free. Even his own most spiritual achievements, such as language and rationality, can turn against him. What are usually taken as uniquely human abilities work against man and, in collusion with the material world, hold man in a vice-grip of destruction. Language leads to silence. Life leads to death. There is possible here no existentially self-authenticating act. Ionesco's vision goes beyond (or perhaps falls short of) existentialism and its doctrine of freedom. Ionesco's man is not free to be other than the kind of death-bound being he is. Transcendence above his situation is impossible. At one point in *Victims of Duty* Choubert says, "After all, I'm only a man," and the Detective replies, "You must be a man to the bitter end" (p. 148). And the bitter end of this man is that he cannot transcend his appointed end through any significant gestures or assertions which bespeak freedom.

One of the most cherished values in Western society is that of the family, where individuals live in community. In the plays we have discussed there is little treatment of this value, but we can discern in the relationship between Choubert and Madeleine what is typical of Ionesco's assumptions at this point. We have seen how Madeleine exists primarily as a mirror reflection of Choubert's changing selves, and we have noted Choubert's lack of genuine knowledge of who Madeleine is and his failure to relate to her in any but highly ego-oriented ways. We are confronted here with a situation which differs from both traditional individualism and modern collectivism. It is not that man is an isolate who cannot relate to others in genuine community. Nor is it that individuals are swallowed up in collectives that tend to rob them of their uniqueness of being. In Ionesco's theatre we are faced with a situation where neither individuality nor community is really possible. Man is not born into a community, nor does he autonomously join a collective. His existence is not described by either of these categories.

The question of how man knows anything poses a considerable problem for Ionesco's man. Based on the evidence in the two plays we have discussed, it seems fairly clear that reason is not a dependable tool by which man comes to terms with his experience. We have seen how man's usual reasoning processes either break down or become demonically threatening to his very existence. The only kind of knowing that Ionesco seems to allow is that ambiguous, intuitive, poetic knowing characteristic of dream. At one point Nicolas d'Eu admits his debt to surrealism in his theory of the theatre, so long as "surrealism is oneirical . . ." (p. 158). This line is in keeping with Ionesco's own theory of the theatre which insists upon its essentially poetic, revelatory function. But this is not to assume that the dramatic imagination delivers revealed truth from some transcendent realm. It is only to suggest that the theatrical presentation (showing forth) of an inner vision comes as near to telling the truth about man as is possible. In the revelation of man through the dramatic imagination a kind of knowledge of man is gained, but such knowledge is not open to translation into propositional terms. The theatrical image is the knowledge, and in this assumption Ionesco agrees with the mainstream of modern poetic theory.

The problem of identity in Ionesco's image of man opens onto another problem, namely whether man has any significant history. Since Choubert's psychological journey back into time failed to find Mallot, the assumption would seem to be that history holds no meaning. If the alternative to historical significance for man is some kind of existential significance, a similar problem emerges. If man has no freedom with which to decide in favor of existence, then it is difficult to locate existential significance for him. Man *is*, in Ionesco's world, but beyond this bare assertion no further judgments can be made with any assurance.

Is Ionesco's world entirely absurd? Is there any meaning which can be asserted or assumed for man which grants him something which might be called humanity? It is difficult to say. We have seen from Ionesco's essays how it is possible for him to experience wonder at the sheer fact of existence, but such moments of "evanescence" are short-lived. In the image of man Ionesco presents, it is difficult to assert even this possibility of self-transcending wonder and joy at being alive. And yet there is the matter of humor. In Ionesco's theatre, humor is not shared by the characters, only by the audience. Confronted with his image of man, we are prompted through irony, situation, pun, tricks of theatre, and all the rest of Ionesco's immensely creative and imaginative dramatic equipment, to laugh at his man. Our laughter is never so self-forgetting as to be totally unaware of the implications for our own existence of what we see and hear. But this "lucid" laughter does grant a kind of self-transcendence over the absurdity of existence as presented in Ionesco's theatre. If we are dealing here with a total theatrical event, our response to the plays is as much a part of the whole as the language and action of the actors. In this sense, then, we can say that Ionesco does assume a kind of possible meaning in existence which is revealed through laughter at life's absurdity.

Ionesco's image of a man absolutely isolated, whose identity "is like that of a vacuum,"[24] who himself is "encircled in a void,"[25] whose language has an unutterable silence at its center, suggests little of value which can be asserted on man's behalf. But this is an imaginative image, the work of a sensibility expressing itself in the theatre. The very act of creative imagination cannot be left entirely aside from what is asserted by the lineaments of the image itself. This image is genuinely had only in a living theatre. Whether a living theatre could be sustained very long in these terms is beside the point. The issue centers in a creative presentation, requiring human life and imagination. We can argue that Ionesco manages with humor and seriousness to present us with an image of man which pushes us back upon ourselves, there to face the metaphysical realities of our own existence.

Contrary to those playwrights who prescribe political or psychological cures for the ills of mankind, Ionesco believes that no program of human manipulation can even ask the right questions of existence:

> In fact, I believe that it is precisely when we see the last of economic problems and class warfare (if I may avail myself of one of the most crashing clichés of our age) that we shall also see that this solves nothing, indeed that our problems are only beginning. We can no longer avoid asking ourselves what we are doing here on earth, and how, having no deep sense of our destiny, we can endure the crushing weight of the material world.[26]

Ionesco asks this question by presenting an image of man being crushed by both his internal world of reason and language and by his external world of fellowmen and the material universe. The answer to the question is left open. But in the anguish, absurdity, indeed laughability, of the image there is a lucidity of vision that claims our attention. And the claim is made with the authenticity of poetic truth.

JEAN GENET

Despite the biting critique of bourgeois society and culture common to all the playwrights of the avant-garde theatre, the others are paragons of bourgeois virtue compared to Jean Genet. In his monumental study of Genet,[1] Jean-Paul Sartre claims that prison made a poet and playwright of him. Whether the relationship between Genet's imprisonment for theft and his literature is strictly causative is not so important as the fact that Genet has incarnated in his own existence much of the antagonistic stance toward bourgeois values and institutions common to the "social protest" interests of his colleagues in the theatre.

In his preface to the 1954 edition of *The Maids*, Genet discusses briefly his concept of the theatre. He expresses considerable dislike for the typical Western theatre and, like Artaud, prefers an Oriental style. Sounding very much like Artaud, though never referring to him, Genet says, "One can only dream of an art that would be a profound web of active symbols capable of speaking to the audience a language in which nothing is said but everything portended."[2] He is disturbed by a theatre which "reflects the visible world too exactly, the actions of men and not Gods," and so he attempts in *The Maids* "to effect a displacement that, in permitting a declamatory tone, would bring theatre into the theatre."[3] The training ground for his theatre would be more akin to a "seminary" than to a "conservatory." It is not surprising, therefore, that he finds great theatrical significance in Christian ritual.

> On a stage not unlike our own, on a platform, the problem was to reconstitute the end of a meal. On the basis of this one particular which is now barely perceptible in it, the loftiest modern drama has been expressed daily for two thousand years in the sacrifice of the Mass. The point of departure disappears beneath the profusion of ornaments and symbols that still overwhelm us. Beneath the most familiar of appearances—a crust of bread—a god is devoured. I know nothing more theatrically effective than the elevation of the host: . . . A performance that does not act upon my soul is vain. It is vain if I do not believe in what I see, which will end—which will never have been—when the curtain goes down. No doubt one of the functions of art is to substitute the efficacy of beauty for religious faith. At least, this beauty should have the power of a poem, that is, of a crime. But let that go.[4]

It is clear that Genet's "poetics" reaches toward both the Western tradition of religious ritual and the tradition of poetic sensibility that rests upon a "willing suspension of disbelief." For our own purposes, Genet's statement is both an invitation and a warning. Ritualized theatre is certainly open to theological criticism, but we must not assume that because Genet finds great theatrical significance in the Mass that he is therefore a crypto-Christian playwright. In wanting to substitute the efficacy of beauty for that of religious faith, he wants to fill a vacuum where faith, once alive, is now dead. Genet is very much within that group of modern playwrights who see the theatre as a substitute for the church.

Genet concludes his comments on the theatre by castigating the isolation brought about by modern theatre. He wishes that the theatre might bring human beings together in a form of genuine communion, if only for an hour or two. Instead, he feels the modern theatre is no more than a diversion begetting dispersion. The only hope might be "A clandestine theatre, to which one would go in secret, at night, and masked, a theatre of the catacombs . . ."[5] While his own popularity with the general public led to his early plays-in-performance being a kind of common celebration of the "faithful," Genet has become commercially successful since he wrote these comments, and a "clandestine" theatre is no longer possible for his own plays, except insofar as the *petit bourgeoisie* attend his theatre secretly expecting pornography and a vicarious experience of vice and perversion. Unfortunately for the bourgeoisie, they find the outcasts of society have the same private dreams and horrors that *les justes* enjoy.

Genet's theatre is certainly no less open-ended as to possible interpretations than that of the other avant-garde playwrights. Despite Sartre's seemingly exhaustive analysis of Genet, highly informed critics differ not only with Sartre but with each other regarding the import of Genet's vision. Professor Pucciani argues that Genet's use of distancing is both an aesthetic and metaphysical device:

> This distance is a strange thing. It is, of course, aesthetic distance. But it is also the metaphysical distance from man to man; the untraversable distance from man to divinity. . . . We are thus placed on the stage, made a part of the performance but after the manner of religious ceremonies. Remoteness is essential to our participation. Without it there would be only sentimentality and diversion. There could be no rigor and there would be no communion.[6]

Thus Pucciani seems to be claiming success for Genet in terms of Genet's own poetics, a theatre in which communion is achieved through transcendence of immediate human involvements. On the other hand, Professor Svendsen argues that Genet is completely bound up in his own private sensibility, a vision which does not open onto general and universal experience:

> Genet spins no theology—at least, not a philosophic, though possibly a kerygmatic one. Genet does not eliminate or replace God or possible conceptions of one, even when we argue that he creates world of inverse order: to invert would argue the existence of the inverted. Therefore, if we may be so coldly cruel and logical, he does not argue the actual order. He keeps silence whereof he does not know, and pours out his power in behalf of the deamons that torment him. . . . he has, like others now lackadaisically lumped together as absurdists, cut off his horizons, limited his possibilities, and forced himself to dwell in auto-kerygma—a theological transvaluation of autoeroticism.[7]

While granting Professor Svendsen's intellectual bias toward the thought of Ludwig Wittgenstein, we can credit him with a significant counter to Pucciani's conviction that Genet's theatre does have both theological and communal aspects. Svendsen's focus upon Genet's private vision, his "auto-kerygma," would seem to eliminate the possibility of the communion experience in this theatre, if not the question of some kind of theological significance.

The critics do agree, implicitly if not explicitly, that Genet's theatre does have a highly ritualistic character. The implications for his obvious trading upon the Christian tradition, while not entirely clear, are nevertheless present. We shall inquire into his theatre in relation to his image of man. A shorter play, *The Maids*, and a longer play, *The Blacks*, will provide the basis of our analysis and discussion.

As *The Maids*[8] begins, we find ourselves listening to a discussion between a woman and her maid. The woman is haughty; the maid, servile. There are some indications in the dialogue that this is a peculiar relationship, but it is not clear just how peculiar until an alarm clock rings. The two women then run into each other's arms and listen for voices or footsteps which would indicate the arrival of Madame. We had thought we had been listening to Madame and Claire, but it turns out that we have been listening to Claire and Solange playing at being Madame and Claire. Claire and Solange are the maids in question, and we learn that virtually every evening they take turns at playing Madame and each other. In this game Claire is never Claire, and Solange is never Solange. Thus each character plays the role of a character who plays a role.[9]

With the interruption of what Claire calls their "ceremony," we begin to piece together something of the identities of these two women. They seem to be sisters, though we are not really sure. They share a garret room together and are visited, in turn, by a young milkman, whose amorous machinations constitute almost their sole relationship with the world beyond their service to Madame. Claire would appear to be the younger of the two, and in some respects she is the more volatile and domineering one. We learn nothing of their backgrounds. In the foreground of their existence is their love-hate relationship to each other and to Madame.

SOLANGE: Go on, be sarcastic, work me up! Go on, be sarcastic! Nobody loves me! Nobody loves us!
CLAIRE: *She* does, *she* loves us. She's kind. Madame is kind! Madame adores us.
SOLANGE: She loves us the way she loves her armchair. Not even *that* much! Like her bidet, rather. Like her pink enamel toilet-seat. And we, can't love one another. Filth . . .

. . .

. . . doesn't love filth. D'you think I'm going to put up with it that I'm going to keep playing this game and then at night go back to my fold-

> ing-cot? The game! Will we even be able to go
> on with it? And if I have to stop spitting on
> someone who calls me Claire, I'll simply choke!
> My spurt of saliva is my spray of diamonds (pp.
> 51 f.).

Thus the ambiguities of their relationship with each other and
Madame gain painful and scabrous expression. Claire sar-
castically ridicules Solange for having failed to go through
with an attempted murder of Madame by choking her in her
sleep. Solange claims, in one breath, that she had intended to
kill Madame in order to free Claire and, in the next breath,
says that if she had succeeded, Claire would have been the
first to turn her in. We learn that Solange had projected her
romanticized version of her attempted crime into the previous evening's game. She, playing Madame, had envisioned
Madame's lover, Monsieur, as a criminal whom she would
follow to Siberia or Devil's Island in the grand manner of the
noble prostitute. Similarly, "this evening" Claire had inter-
jected the "milkman" aspect of their lives into the game by
ridiculing "Claire" for her nocturnal revels with him. Thus
affection, perhaps love, is mingled both in conversation and
in the game with hate and ridicule. These events, accusations,
protestations, claims, aspirations, hopes, fears—all aspects of
identity and relationship—are confusedly intermingled until
we are not at all sure who Claire and Solange are or might be.

When the telephone rings and we learn that Monsieur
has been released from jail, we discover another dimension
of the maids' relationship with Madame. They had sent anon-
ymous letters to the police denouncing Monsieur as a thief in
a gesture of rebellion against Madame. Now this scheme has
backfired and they fear discovery. It becomes Claire's turn to
envision a romantic murder-escape action by poisoning Madame. Her gesture will be partly out of rebellion and partly
out of spite toward Solange and her failure to murder Ma-

dame. As Claire says of Solange, "I'm sick of seeing my image thrown back at me by a mirror, like a bad smell. You're my bad smell" (p. 61). And yet she is dependent upon Solange to bring off the murder:

> You'll help me. And, far away, Solange, if we have to go far away, if I have to leave for Devil's Island, you'll come with me. You'll board the boat. The flight you were planning for him can be used for me. We shall be that eternal couple, Solange, the two of us, the eternal couple of the criminal and the saint. We'll be saved, Solange, saved, I swear to you! (p. 63)

Again, the relationships are complicated by romantic visions and lesbianic overtones. But what comes to inescapable expression is Genet's own vision of "the eternal couple of the criminal and the saint."[10] These two are less potential individuals bound together in Claire and Solange than they are aspects of Genet's image of man in his potential triumph over existence. However, in the case of Claire and Solange there is no triumph.

When Madame finally does return, she discovers the telephone still off the hook, and Solange reveals that Monsieur is free from jail. In her eagerness to join him, Madame refuses the poisoned tea Claire has prepared for her and departs leaving Claire's intention frustrated. At this point Claire decides to resume the "ceremony," and in the end she drinks the tea and dies. Solange is left alone to accept responsibility for the suicide-murder, though she now is as Claire-Madame has described her, the two of them. In her final soliloquy Solange says,

> Madame is dead. Her two maids are alive: they've just risen up, free, from Madame's icy form. All the maids were present at her side—not they themselves, but rather the hellish agony of their names. And all that remains of them to float about Madame's airy corpse is the delicate perfume of the holy

maidens which they were in secret. We are beautiful, joyous, drunk, and free (p. 100).

Of course, they are none of these things. Claire is dead and Solange is ugly, sad, sober, and enslaved to the image of an identity she has never possessed, only reflected through a mirror darkly.

The characters of this play have no relationship to the created order. Genet intends that they shall begin at some distance from what ordinarily appears to be reality. In his early work, *Our Lady of the Flowers,* Genet had said,

> If I were to have a play put on in which women had roles, I would demand that these roles be performed by adolescent boys, and I would bring this to the attention of the spectators by means of a placard which would remain nailed to the right or left of the sets during the entire performance.[11]

That the productions of *The Maids* have not used boys is a mere concession to convention. Genet wishes to eliminate any easy assumptions that natural appearances grant reality. By "derealizing" (Sartre's term) the characters at the outset, Genet brings his *mise en scène* into a supporting relationship with his ritualistic action. By so doing, the question of who is Claire and who is Solange is always undercut by the question of who is a maid, and this question is undercut by the question of who is a woman. This spiral of increasing distance from apparent reality constitutes a metaphysical quest for an understanding of being. But it is a process of negating all appearances of reality in order that the profound unreality of all appearances becomes evident. But for Genet this is a poetic quest, not a philosophical procedure. This process takes place within the realm of the imaginary. In *The Maids* we see the process taking place, but we also feel a tension between the primarily linguistic nature of the quest and the rudiments of dramatic plot that Genet feels are necessary to get his images staged in a theatrical event.

The action of *The Maids* is an interrupted ritual murder of Madame. The intention of the ritual is to exorcise Madame as the daemon who holds the maids captive. But for Genet such a ritual is not a matter of linguistic incantation through which the words "Maid" and "Madame" take on a kind of being. It is as though these words suck their existence from their counterparts in reality, leaving the substance of reality highly in question. Once the words are given shape and gesture through the theatrical event, a further spiral is set in motion downward toward nothingness. The French critic, Marc Pierret, comments,

> Poet of the imaginary, Genet is also a realistic author. All of his power springs from the fact that he is able to make us forget that he is a writer so that he may then drag us to the outermost limits of knowing and not-knowing. Detaching himself from the bitterness and hate he feels for the bourgeois world, Genet uses these very emotions as instruments of meditation on the being and non-being of the Word. But the Word can become meaningful only after it has been stripped of all the feeling society has heaped on it in order to possess it. For Genet poetry is an act of stripping away. He creates death.[12]

At the level of ordinary theatre, *The Maids*, staged in a Louis XV bedroom, laden with plot devices, runs the risk of seeming to be little more than melodrama. But, at the level of linguistic images, the play becomes a terrifying vision of the way in which labels take away the life of their referents, only to end in another kind of death which sucks both body and spirit into its whorl of nothingness.

Genet is fond of the image of a house of mirrors in which the unhappy victims of illusion become entirely bound into a series of reflections and distortions of their own misery. For Genet this image is indicative of existence as he knows it as a marginal member of society. There is no disputing that he projects much of his own interior agony and anger into his poetry and plays, but whether he intends for his characters to portray man's spiritual and existential situation is open to question. Claire and Solange speak of each other as mirror images. We have seen how difficult it is to locate anything approaching solid identity for either of these two unhappy women. They speak of desiring freedom and engage in a ritual exorcism of Madame, the source of their servitude, but they are so bound by the reflections of love and hate in one another that even their gestures toward ritual freedom richochet from situation to situation, night to night, until there is only the "freedom" of death. Because of the ambiguity of their constantly changing roles there is never any assurance that either is in any sense an individual. Nor is there a quality of community about their relationship which might grant authenticity to their individuality. Apart from the repetitious gestures of their game, their existence has no meaning other than the dialectic between fauning servitude and desperate animosity engendered by their relationship with Madame. In their relationships with each other and with Madame all thought and action are reflexive and self-consuming. Appearance gnaws at existence to bare the unreality of appearance only to scab over with another appearance, which again festers and breaks open to a new level of unreality.

Whatever may be Genet's real feelings about man, the image he presents in *The Maids* is of man (or, rather, woman) reduced to his name and that name caught in a linguistic maze of mirror actions which have only destruction as their consequence. We are left sensing that this image feeds not only upon life as we know it, but even upon theatre as a creative act of the human spirit. If nothing more, we are less prone to assume that nominalistic behavior and thought deliver genuine reality for us outside the theatre. But there is a deeper demonic dimension to this vision which seems to grip even the theatre in a destructive grasp that includes all human efforts toward transcendence and meaning. And yet the vision remains as a poetic projection of Genet's highly personal dis-ease. It exists in language, and it can exist as theatre. *The Maids*, as a play, is saved by its plot, though its vision, like the ritual of the maids, is self-consuming in its bent toward destruction of thought and spirit at the boundaries of knowing and not knowing.

Genet solves the tension between ritual and plot in *The Blacks*[13] by eliminating plot almost altogether. At least in reading or seeing the play, we are in no doubt that the central action of the play is a ritual reenactment of the murder of a white woman by a Negro. It is often commented that Genet's plays have a quality of a Black Mass about them, and certainly this was true with *The Maids*. In *The Blacks* Genet has deliberately given this quality a punning turn by creating a play in which Blacks perform a Black Mass with a white victim and before two white audiences. One white audience is a group of Negro actors wearing white masks depicting the stereotyped figures of a colonial government: Queen, Governor, Judge, Missionary, and Queen's Valet. The other white audience is just the audience which has come to see the play. In a prefatory note to the play, Genet says,

> This play, written, I repeat, by a white man, is intended for a white audience, but if, which is unlikely, it is ever performed before a black audience, then a white person, male or female, should be invited every evening. The organizer of the show should welcome him formally, dress him in ceremonial costume and lead him to his seat, preferably in the front row of the orchestra. The actors will play for him. A spotlight should be focused upon this symbolic white throughout the performance.
> But what if no white person accepted? Then let white masks be distributed to the black spectators as they enter the theatre. And if the blacks refuse the masks, then let a dummy be used.[14]

Thus the audience is not only a part of this theatrical event, but it must be, actually or symbolically, a white audience in order that the ritual action be complete.[15]

The play begins with a group of Negroes dancing a Mozart minuet around a catafalque draped with a white cloth. As the Court (the white masks) enters, the dancing stops and Archibald, a kind of master of ceremonies, takes over and introduces the members of the dancing group. He addresses the audience directly, telling us that he and his friends will perform for us this evening. He continues,

> . . . but, in order that you may remain comfortably settled in your seats in the presence of the drama that is already unfolding here, in order that you be assured that there is no danger of such a drama's worming its way into your precious lives, we shall even have the decency—a decency learned from you—to make communication impossible. We shall increase the distance that separates us—a distance that is basic—by our pomp, our manners, our insolence—for we are actors. When my speech is over, everything here—(he stamps his foot in a gesture of rage) here!—will take place in the delicate world of reprobation (p. 12).

No doubt distancing is necessary to a ritual action, and no doubt communication is difficult between two groups which have been so clearly separated and defined apart by color barriers, but the images portrayed communicate at levels much deeper than that announced by Archibald, as Genet well knows. But the ironies of Archibald's speech do not escape us, since we are both "white" and bourgeois. For *les justes*, the theatre is indeed often a matter of "delicate reprobation," but we quickly sense that Archibald's very anger makes the theatre a more real world than that in which we live outside. This "outside" world is represented in the play by an action we learn about in which a Negro traitor is killed and a new hero is sent to Africa in his place. Newport News reports on this "outside" action from time to time, but we must not forget that this "outside" is just as much inside the theatre as the action taking place before our eyes. Genet is working on many levels at once.

We are introduced to some of the characters by Archibald, only to be told that nothing is true about what he has said. He assures us that when he and his colleagues leave the stage that

> ... we are involved in your life. I am a cook, this is a sewing-maid, this gentleman is a medical student, this gentleman is a curate at St. Anne's, this lady ... skip it. Tonight, our sole concern will be to entertain you. So we have killed this white woman. There she lies. ... Oh, I was forgetting, thieves that we are, we have tried to filch your fine language. Liars that we are, the names I have mentioned to you are false (p. 14).

On one level, he seems to be saying simply that in a white society Negroes are servants, medical students, clergymen, and prostitutes—ordinary people. On another level, he reflects common stereotypal conceptions of the Negro as a thief and liar. In consequence, the identities of these characters are both unknown and immaterial. They are functionaries in a ritual action and actors in a theatre, but they are not characters in a drama in the usual sense. The one possible exception to this lack of identity is the couple, Village and Virtue. Village enacts the role of Negro assailant and Virtue is "known" as a prostitute, but more importantly they are in love, or say they want to become so. The ritual demands that their outside lives not become evident and involved, but the lyric quality of their relationship continually breaks in and disrupts the ritual.

On another level, the group as a whole is involved in the ritual, performed before the "white" Court, in order to become identified with the color black. As Archibald says, "The tragedy will lie in the color black! It's *that* that you'll cherish, *that* that you'll attain, and deserve. It's *that* that must be earned" (p. 17). This identity can only be earned by committing a crime for which they will be condemned. They are, as Archibald later says, "like guilty prisoners who play at being guilty" (p. 39). Thus the ritual has the dual purpose of exorcising both their hate of the whites and their sense of guilt at being black. This is not quite the same kind of relationship as existed between the maids and Madame, a love-hate relationship needing ritual enactment and resolution. In *The Blacks* the ritual is aimed at establishing a sense of identity and meaning, on the one hand, and at releasing the guilt felt by those not accepted by the dominant society, on the other hand. Love becomes a possibility only within the black group once it has gained these ritual objectives, as the end of the play discloses. Any kind of positive relationship between the whites and blacks is excluded as a possibility, both within the ritual drama and within the theatre event which the play as a whole defines.

Briefly, the ritual action consists in one of the characters, Diouf (the curate), being invested with a grotesque mask of a blond, smiling, white woman. Village, who had earlier reported "today's" actual murder as having involved an old crone sitting on a dock, begins the ritual murder of a white storekeeper. But, instead of being terrified of her assailant's intentions, the woman is overwhelmed by his superior sexual attractions and invites him into her bedroom, where she is raped and choked to death. This action is constantly being interrupted by the Court and its utterances on other matters, such as stock market quotations. It would be saying too much to claim that this ritual action is unambiguously clear and well defined, but in time it is finished and the Court makes an imaginary pilgrimage into darkest Africa to punish the Blacks for their crime. Locale is never sure, the action is broken by news from Newport News, Village and Virtue keep interjecting their "private" lives, but in the end the Court is killed

off and sent to hell after the Black Queen, Mrs. Felicity, has
verbally vanquished the White Queen. In a sense, there are
two rituals, or two parts to one complicated ritual. First, there
is the ritual crime which will earn the condemnation of the
Court, and second, there is the ritual murder of the Court. It
is not enough ritually to kill one representative of the dominant group; the leaders of that group themselves must also
be murdered. Where does this leave the white audience? We
are being entertained, or are we?

A clue to where we are is indicated in the end of the play
when Village is protesting his love for Virtue.

VILLAGE: But if I take your hands in mine? If I put my
arms around your shoulders—let me—if I hug
you?

VIRTUE: All men are like you: they imitate. Can't you
invent something else?

VILLAGE: For you I could invent anything: fruits, brighter
words, a two-wheeled wheelbarrow, cherries
without pits, a bed for three, a needle that
doesn't prick. But gestures of love, that's harder
. . . still, if you really want me to . . .

VIRTUE: I'll help you. At least, there's one sure thing:
you won't be able to wind your fingers in my
long golden hair . . .
(The black backdrop rises. All the Negroes—
including those who constituted the Court and
who are without their masks—are standing about
a white-draped catafalque like the one seen at
the beginning of the play. Opening measures of
the minuet from *Don Giovanni*. Hand in hand,
Village and Virtue walk toward them, thus turning their backs to the audience. The curtain is
drawn.) (p. 128)

As Village and Virtue rejoin their group, turning their backs
on the audience, their identity has been (perhaps) achieved.
We are left with ours considerably in question. The price of

our entertainment is the realization of separation, a separation intensified because we also do not know how to invent gestures of love.

However, we need to be careful about drawing neat morals. After all, Village and Virtue rejoin a group gathered about a catafalque. Even if the catafalque is only two chairs with a cloth draped over them, as the earlier one had turned out to be, a repetition of the ritual is indicated as a distinct possibility, thus suggesting that it must be repeated if identity is to be maintained. Village may never learn to invent gestures of love; the being he achieves at the close of the ritual may always fall into nonbeing when the trance is broken. We do not know for sure.

In contrast to *The Maids*, the *mise en scène* in *The Blacks* in no way represents anything but an imaginary context for a ritual. There are scaffolds at the back of the stage, at the top of which sits the Court; and part way up, Mrs. Felicity sits and knits when she is not exhorting, voodoo style, all Negroes to incarnate themselves through her. The ritual takes place on a bare stage and the rape-murder takes place behind a screen, since this play is likened to Greek tragedy with its decorum: "The ultimate gesture is performed off stage" (p. 84). Below and in front of the stage sits the white audience. Thus the blacks are caught between fake whites above and real whites below. The fake whites don masks to enact the stereotypes of whites as seen by blacks. The blacks enact a ritual in which they become the stereotypes of blacks as seen by whites. But all are actors playing roles of characters they are not. The audience is at times addressed directly. At one point a member of the audience is asked to come onto the stage and hold a property piece. We are told by Genet's translator that in the Paris production the Court entered from the audience. In these ways the distance is both contracted and expanded between actors and audience. The result of visual, linguistic, emotional, gestural varieties of levels is at times very confusing. But the end result is a total theatrical event such as Artaud hoped for. At one point Archibald angrily insists that "this is the theater, not the street. The theater, and drama, and crime" (p. 58). It is, of course, a fake crime that is committed, but the intention is certainly one of cruelty, dislocation, evocation of an image like a plague which has either death or health as its outcome.

Genet's language in *The Blacks* is a language of hate, anger, disgust, and rejection. Archibald calls Village on his use of the term "father," a term of relationship and perhaps of endearment. Village replies, "And what do you suggest I call the male who knocked up the negress who gave birth to me?" Archibald returns with,

> Dammit, do the best you can. Invent—if not words, then phrases that cut you off rather than bind you. Invent, not love, but hatred, and thereby make poetry, since that's the only domain in which we're allowed to operate (p. 26).

When Diouf has been masked as the white woman, Virtue greets him with a litany, chanted, the stage directions tell us, "the way litanies of the Blessed Virgin are recited in church, in a monotone."

Litany of the Livid

Livid as a t.b. death rattle,
Livid as the droppings of a man with jaundice,
Livid as the belly of a cobra,
Livid as their convicts,
Livid as the god they nibble in the morning,
Livid as a knife in the night,
Livid . . . except: the English, Germans and Belgians,
who are red . . . livid as jealousy.
Hail, the livid! (p. 57)

Thus the ritual object of their hatred is greeted, and Village

is encouraged to work himself up to his act of revenge which
"will save him." This kind of language is aimed at evoking
the image of the black, standing in hatred before his white
counterpart.

> In the world of prelogical thought, dream, and myth, lan-
> guage becomes incantation instead of communication; the
> word does not signify a concept but magically conjures up a
> thing—it becomes a magical formula. Desire and love express
> themselves in the wish for possession through identification and
> incorporation of the beloved object. Incantation, magical
> substitution, and identification are the essential elements of
> ritual. It is the use of language as incantatory magic—the ob-
> jectification of words—that makes Genet's theatre, in spite
> of its harshness and scabrous content, into a truly poetical
> theatre, a translation, as it were, of Baudelaire's *Fleurs du
> Mal* into dramatic imagery.[16]

Genet does evoke a thing, in this case a black, but the ritual
in this play is not aimed at identification with the whites,
rather the opposite. It is clear that Genet intends his language
to evoke a thing, not a life.

The only relief from the language of separation and
hatred comes in Village's reminiscence of the first time he
saw Virtue:

> When I beheld you, you were walking in the rain, in high
> heels. You were wearing a black silk dress, black stockings,
> patent leather pumps and were carrying a black umbrella.
> Oh, if only I hadn't been born into slavery! I'd have been
> flooded with a strange emotion, but we—you and I—were
> moving along the edges of the world, out of bounds. We
> were the shadow, or the dark interior, of luminous creatures
> . . . When I beheld you, suddenly—for perhaps a second—
> I had the strength to reject everything that wasn't you, and
> to laugh at the illusion. But my shoulders are very frail. I was
> unable to bear the weight of the world's condemnation. And
> I began to hate you when everything about you would have
> kindled my love and when love would have made men's con-

tempt unbearable, and their contempt would have made my
love unbearable. The fact is, I hate you (pp. 35 f.).

Even a love lyric is twisted into hate language under the
burden of felt condemnation and guilt. The moment of release we feel in the beginning of this reminiscence is soon
turned into an even crueler sense of separation because of the
reflex in Village's emotion. Genet's language, together with
his *mise en scène* and ritual action, conspires to evoke an image which (as one of the characters says it will) sets our
teeth on edge.

But does Genet evoke what might be called a living image?
Certainly his play lives as a theatrical event. He says he is
addressing himself to the color black as something which a
black man is supposed to possess. Are Negroes black? This
question is never answered in any final way. Certainly the
play is not primarily, if at all, about race relations or the
colonial problem, though it can be taken in either of these
ways. Genet seems to be interested in evoking, through ritual
incantation, language, gesture, and movement, an image of
something essentially nonliving: a black. This is not to say
that in the process we are not confronted with many aspects
of contemporary society, man's relationships with his fellowman and with himself, etc. But it is to say that Genet's vision is not of living society, but of a reflection of the color of
those who are dead so far as society is concerned: criminals,
Negroes, homosexuals, i.e., Genet's candidates for sainthood.
Sartre insists that Genet himself is a dead man. "If he appears
to be still alive, it is with the larval existence which certain
peoples ascribe to their defunct in the grave. All his heroes
have died at least once in their life."[17] While Ionesco's characters are constantly threatened with death and contingency,
Genet's characters seem never to have been alive. To be sure,
they are emanations of Genet's imagination, and in this sense
not alive. But, more than this, his blacks are engaged in an es-

sentially futile ritual effort to discover their color, a meaning-less, dead aspect of what might have once lived as a man. Here indeed is the tragedy, an image of men reduced to an action the end of which is only the achievement of something with-out life.

Genet calls *The Blacks* a "clown show." Must we take a clown show seriously? Esslin suggests that we could not take it at all if it were not for the clownery and parody of the ritual presented: white audiences could not bear it otherwise.[18] To be sure, the Court play their roles with enthusiasm as they parody the stereotyped responses of whites to Negroes as projected by Negroes. Irony runs deep throughout, produc-ing a dark humor. And the general "fool-around" quality of much of the dialogue and action seems to be confirmed in Archibald's last speech in which he thanks his fellow actors for their performances. He continues,

> The time has not yet come for presenting drama about noble matters. But perhaps they suspect what lies behind this ar-chitecture of emptiness and words. We are what they want us to be. We shall therefore be it to the very end, absurdly (p. 126).

In this speech the clowning is at once confirmed and turned to a serious end. Genet would like his rituals to pertain to the acts of gods and not of men. In his thinking, Western society is not yet ready for such a return to the theatrical roots of the tradition. In the meanwhile, sham rituals will have to do for sham men, men who are stereotyped by their society and must live in terms of such false images. In *The Blacks* Genet has tried to suggest that behind the "architecture of emptiness and words" there lies a whole world which is black, but he knows, and we know, that such a world does not in fact exist —it is an emanation of his imagination.

And yet the power of his presentation of a ritualized vision of meaning and identity, freedom and being, leaves us with a profound unrest concerning our own easy assumptions about the validity and security of the world we inhabit.

> Genet's plays are traps. He turns the theatre into a Black Mass . . . Thus as the real world recedes, where controls of sense, fact and knowledge are possible, we are left abandoned in a pit of the imagination where we must once again re-invent knowledge from the new data of our disturbed senses.[19]

In Genet's vision such "re-invention" must take a ritual form. It is at this point, of course, that his vision comes into serious conflict with other religious conceptions of how man relates himself to a transcendent realm of meaning and value. At the very least, we can say that Genet reminds us of the significance of ritual for an existence which aims at living deeper than the level of brittle lucidity so much affirmed in modern emancipated society. But, at the same time, we cannot avoid the failure of his vision to place us in contact with life.

Perhaps this is too strong a judgment. Genet is projecting his vision of ritualized existence upon the stage in a theatrical event. What we may take away from the event, what we may be prompted to discover about our own lives in the light of his vision, is our business and not his. But even if his vision of existence is precisely one of "lies covering lies, fantasies battening upon fantasies, nightmares nourished by nightmares within nightmares,"[20] it is nevertheless a vision, an image, of man's deep dis-ease which cannot be easily neglected. Genet's image is of man in revolt who must invent ritual patterns to enable him to come to some kind of terms with an existence forced upon him from outside. The end of the revolt is death.

ARTHUR ADAMOV

Exhibitionist, self-exorcist, public confessor to private guilt—Arthur Adamov is all of these and more. His private odyssey toward the theatre and, for him, its therapeutic benefits is documented by this highly self-aware and tortured spirit in several statements, which reveal much of the origin and hidden motives of his plays. His immediate reasons for turning to the theatre, after considerable journalistic and literary efforts in other directions, turn upon two events in the mid-forties. One was a thorough reading of Strindberg, particularly *A Dream Play*. He was stimulated by his study to follow Strindberg's method of theatre and was helped to discover the raw materials for theatre in simple, ordinary street events. *Bribes*, fragments of theatre, began to collect in his mind and were brought to focus in one such event. One day Adamov happened on a blind man asking for alms. Two girls came by at just that moment singing a popular song, "I closed my eyes, it was wonderful." In their carelessness, they bumped into the blind beggar and passed on unconcerned. This brief event prompted Adamov to declare, "*C'est cela le théâtre, c'est cela que je veaux faire.*"[1] To show in a theatrical event, as largely and visibly as possible, human solitude and the absence of communication—this became Adamov's goal in turning to the theatre. His first play, *La Parodie*,[2] was three years and multiple versions in arriving at completion.

While Adamov is unwilling to speak further about his reasons for turning to the theatre,[3] we can yet discern in earlier statements much of his own inner condition which gave rise to the contents of his first plays. Just after World War II, Adamov became editor of a short-lived little magazine, *L'Heure Nouvelle*. Included in the first issue was his article, "Une Fin et un Commencement," in which he declared:

> From whatever point he starts, whatever path he follows, modern man comes to the same conclusion: behind its visible appearances, life hides a meaning that is eternally inaccessible to penetration by the spirit that seeks for its discovery, caught in the dilemma of being aware that it is impossible to find it, and yet also impossible to renounce the hopeless quest.[4]

This, for Adamov, is the tragic situation of modern man, for whom the name of God no longer has any meaning and for whom the old religious rites are dead upon the ash heaps of modern Western history. In the late thirties, Adamov himself had become this man, and his only means of dealing with his condition was confession. In a work of that title, *L'Aveu*, Adamov disclosed the contents of his "private terrors," which were later to be exorcised through his plays.

In the middle portion of *L'Aveu*, translated as "The Endless Humiliation," Adamov states:

> Of course I am an exhibitionist. But that is not the point. The point is: I exorcise myself. By confessing my disease, by revealing it true physiognomy, I perform the gesture—apparently in reverse, but identical in purpose—of primitive man donning his sacramental mask. . . . By expressing my disease, I disengage myself from it.[5]

The disease of which he speaks is his own neurotic state of conscious guilt and separation from himself and his fellowman. He needs to "expiate a fault" which has fallen on his very flesh. "But," he says, "the flesh is only a link in the endless chain of realities symbolizing each other. We must discover what is hidden behind the last of such symbols."[6] His method of dealing with his neurosis is one of "both indictment and apology at once." His confession functions as a judgment upon "a phenomenon that arrests man's development and risks steeping him forever in an endless stagnation."[7] But, at the same time, Adamov is aware that his neuroses, like other men's, "grants its victim a peracute lucidity inaccessible to the so-called normal man. . . ."[8] This lucidity begins at the recognition that "neurosis is tangent to both sanctity and madness at their common point: the *idée fixe*, the obsession."[9] Adamov's obsession is a guilt bound up with "the mystery of sex," and his relationships with women are the means by which he plumbs the depths of his own being in order to discover the meaning of his separation.

In a harrowing account of his earlier experiences, Adamov tells us of his desire to be humiliated by women, "and by women only, because women are the Other, the stranger par excellence—the contrary of myself."[10] Since woman is the symbol of all reality not himself, he must pass beyond even this symbol to a place "lower than that which is low." This woman "possesses the attraction of the abyss."

> Thus fatally has woman appeared to me in the guise of the eternal prostitute, her face painted, her eyes blank, and I have followed her into all those places where misery is a commonplace. . . .
> I have tried everything I could to relieve the passion that devours me.
> . . . but confronted with the futile multiplication of the images of lust, I have found only anguish, unspeakable solitude.[11]

His futile quest led Adamov to the realization that even our

Cf
Beckett

language already speaks of man's solitude. "The prefix *ex-*
implies a movement rejecting from the center toward the
exterior. Existence signifies: to be outside. By the mere fact
that he *exists*, man is already an exile, expelled, hence set outside everything."[12] Thus at the bottom of the dialectic between himself and woman there is only anguished solitude
for Adamov, but if it is his, then it is man's.

In a remarkable statement linking his own anguish to that
of all men, Adamov says,

> The overwhelming evidence must become apparent to
> all eyes: This fault is not ultimately *my* fault, it transcends
> me, greater than even the sickness within me. I want to make
> this truth contagious, virulent: every private fault, every in-
> dividual guilt, whether the guilty person is conscious of it or
> not, transcends the individual to identify itself with the fault
> of all men everywhere and forever—the great original pre-
> varication which is named Separation.[13]

But it is his own "peracute" awareness of his fault which
grants him an intensity of particular insight, and thus a vision
of man's universal situation.[14] It is this vision of exile, solitude,
anguish, separation, which we see being revealed in his plays.

If his quest, as disclosed in *L'Aveu*, did not fully release
Adamov from his neurosis, it did at least teach him something of the gestural dimension of life, and this later came
to concrete expression in the plays.

> Imprisoned in the obscurity of my flesh, I have required
> the lure of woman to penetrate the true meaning of humilia-
> tion. But now I know this devouring sentiment must be
> transferred to the sacred terror of the entire unknown which
> lives within and also limits me.
>
> I have fostered the love of the beast that I am. I have at-
> tempted to preserve that beast from various dangers by luna-
> tic gestures. I must now learn to detach myself from this
> swarm of desires, to untie the knot which was strangling my
> life. But the fact remains that this agitation has taught me

the meaning of gesture, the sacred forgotten necessity according to which every movement of thought, in order to achieve reality and to be empowered with life, must be translated into, must echo the gesture corresponding to it in the universe of symbols.[15]

With such an understanding of the relationship between human gestures (and these can be taken to include the full range of physical and linguistic gesturing evident in theatre), it is not surprising that Adamov's plays reveal a relationship between his theatre and that proposed by Antonin Artaud. Adamov was a great friend of Artaud, and thus it is to be expected that when he finally turned to the theatre as a means of expressing his vision of existence, Adamov should quite naturally demonstrate the influence of Artaud. Adamov speaks of having been nourished by *The Theatre and Its Double*.[16] He also follows Artaud in the latter's rejection of the psychological orientation of much modern theatre. But it is of particular interest that in 1939 Adamov was already speaking of the significance of gestures as a means by which man relates himself to his environment and even to ultimate reality. And for Adamov such gestures include physical acts and movement as well as prayer. He tells us of private rituals in which he touches the ground, then wood, and then lights a match, all in sequence to "protect" himself. His relationship to the natural world is disclosed in a brief prayer of praise:

> Wood of the tree of life, in touching you I touch the solidified witness of the great vertical flow of desire, the stratified sign of the clear blood's ascension from the abyss toward the light.
>
> Wood patient as life itself, the slow petrifying agent of forms, you grow so gently that your flesh assuages even human pain.[17]

And in another prayer of petition we hear Adamov addressing himself (as representative modern man) to the dark powers threatening existence.

I am afraid, and from the depths of my fear rises a pitiful prayer, the heavy stammering of anguish: "Obscure powers, forces of shadow fastened on the surface of myself, take pity on my desperate efforts, on the frenzied energy I unremittingly expend with the single purpose of appeasing you. Beyond the movements of my guilty hands—to satisfy you they obey the meticulous fury of all things subject to you. I pledge in sacrifice to you all the time of my life, my heart which beats throughout duration. I give you my time as the most precious of all human treasures, the only gift I can never have back again. In return my need, my demand is not great. I do not ask that the threat which weighs upon me be repealed, but only that it be a little lightened, a little postponed."[18]

While it may be true that Adamov's early plays are "an exorcism of private terrors,"[19] it is nevertheless also true that his vision speaks to our time. That Adamov has now turned away from this vision to the subject of social justice, seen through Marxist eyes, is less significant than the recognition that his early work "remains a very profound insight into the workings of the human mind and retains the power of all deeply felt poetic statements."[20] We shall inquire into this perception of an image of man in terms of two plays: his second play, *L'Invasion*, and a later, shorter play, *Professor Taranne*.

L'Invasion[21] is in many ways different from Adamov's other early plays. In this play the characters are more nearly recognizable human beings than in his first play, *La Parodie*, for instance. In that play most of the characters are known by generic names: L'Employé, N., Le Journaliste, etc. They are little more than ciphers reflecting a Kafkaesque delimitation of personal identity. But in *L'Invasion* we find a mixture of named and generic characters: Pierre, Agnès, Tradel, La Mère, Le Premier Venu, etc. While these characters may stand for something more than themselves, something allegorical, they are at least more than "algebraic figures."[22]

The central character of the play is Pierre, whose life has been invaded by a mysterious manuscript left to him by his deceased friend, Jean, brother to Pierre's wife, Agnès. Pierre's whole life is bound up with the task of deciphering this manuscript, which is nearly illegible and becoming invisible. There seems to be almost no end to the pages of Jean's masterpiece. The problem lies in being able to decide the exact words in any given phrase, and once this is secured there remains the problem of putting the phrase into some kind of intelligible relationship with the whole mass of writing. Endless as the job appears to be, Pierre devotes himself to it with a boundless passion. His friend, Tradel, is engaged in the task with him, but the two men differ radically in their approach to the manuscript. Pierre meticulously studies out each word, while Tradel depends on what he considers to be his inerrant intuitive sense of the meaning he discerns in the fragments on which he works. Tradel is interested in publishing what they find, but Pierre will have none of it. When he refuses to take interest in possible readers who, like Tradel, will appreciate the beauty of Jean's expression, Tradel accuses him of being afraid of himself, afraid to risk public censure for inadequate handling of felt responsibility.

What Tradel fails to understand, and of which Pierre himself may be unconscious, is that the latter is a type of the modern man tragically caught in the quest for meaning, the end of which is never to be found. The manuscript assumes the nature of that meaning "eternally inaccessible to penetration by the spirit that seeks for its discovery" of which Adamov had spoken in his article, "Une Fin et un Commencement." As the play progresses, we become less and less sure that Jean ever knew what he was writing. The assertion is never made that he, like a poet-priest, was somehow a mediator of transcendent meaning, but the way is open for such an hypothesis. What remains clear is that the manuscript exercises a power over Pierre's life that he cannot break, either by giving up the project or by completing it.

Pierre finally rejects Tradel's help entirely and retires to meditate upon language itself. The struggle toward understanding has led him to question the meaning of everything said by anyone, including himself. At one point he cries out:

> Why does one say: "he arrives?" Who is "he," what does he want of me? Why does one say "by" land? Why not "at" or "on"? I have lost too much time reflecting on these things. What I need is not the sense of words but their volume and their moving body. I won't search anymore. I will wait in silence, motionless. I will become very attentive. I must leave as quickly as possible.[23]

And so Pierre forsakes all communal effort at gaining understanding and retreats for two weeks in his room apart (offstage). When he finally returns, Agnès has left him for Le Premier Venu. In despair, he tears up the manuscript and retreats again. At the end of the play Tradel finds him dead in his room.

The two principal women in Pierre's life, his mother and his wife, are in many ways emanations of Adamov's earlier image of woman. We see Pierre's character develop in relationship to these two women, although they remain less well defined than he. La Mère is a generic type who turns up in several of Adamov's plays, as for instance in *Tous contre Tous*[24] and *Les Retrouvailles*.[25] Her relationship to Pierre in *L'Invasion*, clearly a "silver cord" relationship, is symbolized by her armchair in his apartment. At first her chair is located to one side, but by the end of the play she has moved her chair into the center of the stage. Her place in Pierre's life traces a similar pattern. She is at first merely solicitous for his welfare, worrying over his eyes as he strains to read the manuscript, and taking his part in his arguments with Tradel. We begin to discover something of her sinister character when we see her conspiring with Le Premier Venu to lure Agnès out of the home and away from Pierre. While Pierre is in solitude in his room, it is his mother who takes him his food, though she does not converse with him. In the last act, she knows that he is about to come out of his room, but when Agnès returns to borrow the typewriter La Mère does not tell her that Pierre is due out, and so Agnès goes away again without seeing him. La Mère remains dominant in her chair to the end, while Pierre returns to his room to die.

La Mère tidies up the apartment while Pierre is meditating in his room. She piles up all the sheets of the manuscript and covers them with a cloth. She also covers Agnès' typewriter so that it is no longer in sight. These actions seem inconsequential until we realize that one aspect of woman, as Adamov has described in her in *L'Aveu*, is the classical aspect of woman who represents both birth and death. La Mère represents both of these for Pierre, and her tidying up actions are mere preliminary actions for his death. We have noted that he dies in his room. This room is located at the center rear of the stage. By the last act La Mère's chair has assumed a position directly in front of the door to Pierre's room. His isolation, and indeed his whole quest for understanding the manuscript, takes on the quality of a religious quest pursued in hermitic isolation. As he returns to his "cave" to die, he is symbolically returning to the womb of the Terrible Mother of classic mythology. That such an interpretation of La Mère's relationship to Pierre is justified is borne out by his relationship to Agnès, the other pole of Adamov's woman.

Agnès is the one who types up the deciphered bits of the manuscript. She is the instrument of what communication between the manuscript and potential readers might be possible. Things are always messy when she is around, but we have the feeling that genuine possibilities for understanding and meaning are present when she is there. But as Pierre increasingly withdraws from relationship with her and everyone else, her creative possibilities are attenuated and are easily transferred, both sexually and spiritually, to Le Premier Venu (The First One Who Comes Along). When she returns to borrow the typewriter, we learn that her lover's business is failing because he is ill and that she has had to take over. Thus her messiness and this new situation combine to suggest that disintegration is always a possibility with her as well as renewal. But in her relationship to Pierre renewal is always the dominant possibility, whether he realizes it or not. He does realize it when he returns from his isolation to learn that she has just been there and gone off again. He comments to his mother that he and Agnès could have made a new beginning on the manuscript if only she had stayed to help him. But this possibility had been finally frustrated by La Mère.

We are left with Pierre as the dominant image of man who must struggle to wrest meaning from his existence, but who dies if he gives up the quest. His relationships with his mother and wife, his friendship with Tradel, all his existence is brought under the one controlling sense of responsibility he feels to his task of deciphering the manuscript. If his mother and wife are in some sense allegorical characters and if their relationships with each other and with him signify something mythical, he is unaware of all this. The drama of La Mère's gaining dominance in his life as a symbol of the Terrible Mother quite misses his awareness. The spiritual task consumes him and finally destroys him. In rejecting human relationships he must feed only upon his own resources. When these fail, he dies. What the humans in his life might do in his absence or how they might feel about him is not his concern. That his death might be taken as a kind of victory for the hieratic nature of his mother does not interest him. All his human relationships become unimportant in the face of his self-appointed task.

Pierre's world is essentially the apartment we see as the stage set. We do hear of refugees crossing the border, indicating a certain state of disruption in the body politic. This state of affairs in the outside world looms large in several of Adamov's other plays, but in *L'Invasion* there is only a hint of what may be true of the disorder of the world in general. The world of the apartment is certainly disordered until La Mère succeeds in getting rid of Agnès. Esslin suggests that the disorder of the apartment, graphically displayed in the incredible profusion of the manuscript sheets, reflects the internal disorder of the lives of the characters.[26] But this device of the *mise en scène* does more than merely reflect a mental state of the characters. Adamov is most clearly the disciple of Artaud at just this point where his stage becomes precisely a space to be filled. And what is used to fill the stage is also significant—the manuscript plus the large pacing movements of the central characters. They almost wade through the manuscript, and in Act IV when Pierre tears up the sheets he literally becomes swamped in paper. Thus the stage scene itself becomes an image of an invaded universe through which man must make his way. In leaving this particular scene, Agnès seems to carry its disintegrative aspects with her. In imposing her order upon it, La Mère seems to take upon herself the destructive possibilities of this world. Pierre's relationship to his universe is ambivalent. He can neither meaningfully cope with it nor successfully withdraw from it. He can chip away at the mass to gather bits of information, though not meaning. In rejecting his universe by tearing up the manuscript, he seems merely to increase the deadening mass, which in turn forces him into isolation and death.

Adamov's characters do not really communicate with one another. Human understanding is very problematic. He consciously creates a dialogue in this play which makes the characters speak past each other. In doing so, he thought he had discovered a new means of presenting the isolation and loneliness of man. Unfortunately, for him, he discovered that others before him, notably Chekhov, had used the same device.[27] There is no doubt, however, that language is de-emphasized in *L'Invasion*. Again, Adamov is following Artaud in departing from the tradition of a literary theatre in order to stress the elements of spectacle and gesture. As Pronko says, "Instead of cracking and exploding dramatically, as does Ionesco's language, instead of dropping 'like leaves, like sand,' in an intense lyric overflow as does Beckett's, Adamov's dialogue simply drags along."[28] While this judgment is true, it does not gainsay the importance of depressed dialogue for Adamov's image of man. We can only assume that Adamov has the poetic talent to write differently if he so desires. In writing for the theatre a dialogue that "drags along," he is thereby intensifying an image which sees man unable to transcend his situation through flights of language. We must also note that it is precisely the language of the manuscript that is so problematic for Pierre. No single word is unambiguously identifiable and thus capable of carrying a precise meaning. A language which does not communicate, which limps along, which is even obscure in being written down, is a language that intensifies Adamov's vision of man who cannot do without language, but who also cannot fulfill his life through language.

The temptation is to see in Pierre simply a reflection of Adamov's private terrors as revealed in *L'Aveu*. For instance, it is clear that Pierre is the only character having a genuine vocation in existence and, therefore, something of an identity that can be discerned in the light of his work. The other characters are much less well defined. The two principal women combine to form the bipolar image of woman Adamov projected in his "confession." This leaves an image of man which is predominantly an image of male. Who woman might be herself, or who man and woman together might be in their common humanity, is a matter of conjecture. But despite the male orientation of Adamov's vision in *L'Invasion*, we can take Pierre in the broadest possible terms and see in him an image which goes beyond Adamov's private needs for literary expression and exorcism of his neurosis.

Pierre is not free. Esslin suggests that in marrying Agnès he married the legacy of her brother's manuscript. This may in a sense be so, but the internal evidence of the play simply presents Pierre caught in a sense of responsibility toward the manuscript. We have seen how he can neither fully decipher it nor freely leave it. Pierre is presented as a member of a group which is engaged with him in the task he personally feels most responsible for. His sense of responsibility, with its attendant compulsions and pressures upon Agnès, together with his method of procedure, in time drives a wedge between him and his colleagues. An open question is whether he willingly withdraws from community or whether he is forced into withdrawal by his commitment. While his individuality is heightened in his withdrawal, we do not see much evidence of it because he is in isolation in his room off stage, and eventually completely isolated in death. There are several ambiguities about the source of the manuscript itself, and we are left with a feeling that genuine transcendence might be symbolized here, but we are not sure. Pierre brings what powers of reason he has to bear on his task, but they are inadequate to fathom the manuscript. In time he gives up language itself to see if some message attendant upon the sheer mass and form of words will come to him. It doesn't. What revelation from Jean, or beyond, might be possible in the manuscript, or finally in language itself, escapes Pierre. He is man *in situ*, without a history, without a future except as his task be pursued. The meaning of his existence is the non-meaning of the manuscript which has invaded his life, leaving him an "occupied territory" without even a "provisional gov-

ernment" which can administrate within the tension presented
by an unfulfillable and inescapable task.

The difficulty of composition which characterized Adamov's first attempts to write for the theatre was radically overcome when he wrote *Professor Taranne*.[29] This work, the
nearly verbatim transposition of a dream, took only two days
to shape into its present form. Among his early plays, *Professor Taranne* is almost the only one which Adamov now
feels was a good play, because he made no effort to allegorize
its elements.[30] Everything that happens to Professor Taranne in the play happened to Adamov in his dream, with the
single exception that when the Professor cries, "I am Professor Taranne," Adamov had cried in his dream, "Je suis l'au-
teur de *La Parodie*!"[31] This brief play also had the salutary
effect upon Adamov as a writer of demanding that he pay
close attention to details. Since he received a letter in his dream
which had a stamp bearing the royal lion of Belgium, he had to
repeat this fact in the play. Thus he was, as he says, led out of
a "pseudo-poetic *no man's land*" and forced to call things by
their name.[32] But his sortie through dream to the "real world"
was short-lived. He had interrupted the writing of *Le Sens de
la Marche*[33] to write *Professor Taranne*, and it was not until
he had written *Tous contre Tous* and *Les Retrouvailles* that
he established himself in the conventions of theatre realism
with *Le Ping-Pong*[34] (translated as *Ping Pong*). All of the
early plays before *Ping Pong*, except *Professor Taranne*,
share a similar ambiguity as to locale. We have already noted
the frequent use of cipher-like characters named as generic
types. The shift in *Professor Taranne*, while not large, is indicative of what was to come by way of social realism. Our
concern lies with the image of man which *Professor Taranne* projects as both dream and reality.

The play opens with Professor Taranne standing before
a police precinct inspector trying to justify himself for charges

of indecent exposure on a beach. He cannot understand why the police do not recognize him, and if not his face at least his name as an important professor and dean of the faculty at the university. It seems that the police report has come from children who saw him on the beach. None of his accomplishments impress the officer, who only wants him to sign a statement of his guilt. To all the questions the police ask, Taranne responds with affirmation about his importance in the academic world. We learn that he has lectured in Belgium, where he was more readily appreciated than at home, that he is miserly with his time and known by all manner of important people. When he asks the police to bring in any of a number of witnesses to identify him, a Lady Journalist suddenly enters looking for another man. Taranne thinks he recognizes her, though she does not recognize him. Soon, two gentlemen also enter in the midst of a serious, though ambiguous, conversation. Again, there is failure of recognition. The First Gentleman says quite simply, "I don't know you, sir." Taranne had thought he recognized them as two of his students, but they have no idea who he is and cannot testify as to his identity. This exchange is no more than concluded when a Society Lady and two more gentlemen enter. She immediately recognizes him as Professor Menard, whom Taranne resembles. His hopes are shattered as again recognition is not forthcoming which would enable him to justify himself in the face of the police charges. The first scene ends with all the other characters leaving the stage to the distraught Taranne. When he realizes what has happened, he hurries out into the hall and can be heard shouting: ". . . I was supposed to sign a declaration . . . and . . . I haven't done it . . . (terrified) And yet they could not have gone out. One of us would have seen them. I don't understand . . ." (p. 137). When he returns to the stage, the scene has shifted to the office of his hotel.

In the second scene, Taranne is faced with another police charge, this time with leaving papers in a bathing cabin on the beach. His accusers are two policemen from another precinct who know nothing of the first charge. In trying to clear himself of leaving trash in the cabin, he discloses that in the past two days that he has gone swimming he has not taken a cabin and has instead undressed on the beach. He tells of the difficulty of keeping his shirttail down to avoid condemning glances from his fellow bathers. As evidence, the policemen produce a notebook which Taranne recognizes as his own and one which he has filled from cover to cover with notes for future lectures. But the notebook is empty, except for a couple of pages at either end. He recognizes the handwriting as his own, but he cannot decipher what is written. In trying to explain why he did not take a bathing cabin, he claims that he left his money at home and cannot bear the thought of retracing his steps. The time loss would be too great for a man who must use all his spare time for his work. He cannot think or write while walking. He immediately reverses himself in trying to explain the illegibility of his handwriting by saying that he writes while walking and thus scribbles. He finds himself fumblingly resorting to images of the absent-minded professor as an excuse for his inability to justify himself while the policemen walk out, leaving him muttering to himself. Again, he fails to sign a statement as to his guilt, though in this scene he had claimed to have already signed one such statement for the previous charge.

We learn more of who Taranne thinks he is when his sister, Jeanne, brings him a letter from Belgium. The Hotel Manageress had just brought in a scroll which had been left for him and he is studying it rolled out on the floor when Jeanne enters. He tells her the scroll is a map of the seating arrangements on a large ocean liner and that his place is marked for the head table. He has no memory of having booked passage on a liner. As he says, "You don't travel from France to Belgium by sea, as far as I know." Jeanne agrees with him, but turns to the letter she has brought. The letter is from an important professor in the Belgian university where Taranne has already lectured. In the letter the professor explains why he cannot arrange for Taranne to lecture there again. It seems that not only has Taranne offended his colleague by failing to take notice of the latter's sick wife, but he has offended the university by his lectures. They were too long, of unequal quality, and clearly plagiarized from a well-known work by Professor Menard. Taranne is crushed, and when Jeanne leaves and the Manageress takes away the furniture, Taranne hangs up the scroll on the back wall and studies it. It is completely blank. After a moment's pause, Professor Taranne, with his back to the audience, begins to take off his clothes.

In the course of his disclaimers of guilt and protestations of eminence within the university world, Professor Taranne discloses himself to be an exceedingly self-centered man. He has no relationships with anyone which would indicate concern and interest in others. Except insofar as the actions of others directly concern what he thinks is his own welfare, he is totally unconcerned with them. The one possible exception might be his sister, Jeanne. He does relate to her as something of an equal, but her essential relationship to him is merely that of the bearer of his final betrayal as unself-knowing at best, and as carping hypocrite at worst. We know nothing of her as a person; she is the last in a devastating series of mediators of self-knowledge to Taranne.

We have noted how concerned Taranne is with time. This is his only relationship to the cosmos in which he exists. His concern with time further accentuates his self-regard. He thinks of himself as an exceedingly busy man, whose small amount of time must be used with both discretion and efficiency. And yet he takes pride in his long lectures. He has no regard for the urgencies of his students nor of his fellow professors. When accused of failing to post the time of his lectures in the Belgian university and thereby forcing his colleagues to hastily reschedule their lectures, he insists to his sister that they were only too glad to accommodate him. When students find they must leave early or arrive late, he insists that they are only too glad to have even a part of his lectures. Time is an expression of his own interests, not a resource to be used judiciously for the sake of the needs and interests of others.

The kind of dialectical relationships between Taranne's self-identification and that granted him by others, between his concept of time and that of others, between his defense for one accusation and that for another, is underscored by the *mise en scène*. As in a dream, the locales of the several incidents merge into each other. Nothing is certain about the physical arrangements of Taranne's universe. When the Lady Journalist enters, she complains about the heat and asks that a window be opened. In the next minute, the first two gentlemen enter and are wearing heavy winter clothing and make no comment on the weather. Whatever value Adamov himself may attach to indicating Belgium and France as definitive geographical entities, the actual locale of the action is never sure. The stage directions tell us that the first scene begins in a police station, but there are only a desk and some files to indicate this. The two characters in the background, a woman file clerk and a dark young man who goes to sleep sitting astride a chair, give no help in clarifying the situation either of the action or of Taranne's identity. This scene melts into the hotel office, which in turn simply becomes an empty stage where the Professor begins to enact the indecent exposure he has been accused of committing on the beach. No definitions are sure—neither for identity nor time nor place.

It is by no means clear whether Professor Taranne is a free agent confronted with a monstrous conspiracy of circumstances bent upon his destruction or whether he is a fraud by some inner compulsion, who is at last exposed for what he really is. That he is alone is undoubted. He shares in no meaningful community with anyone. Despite his claims for his university standing, and perhaps because of them, he is revealed as an individual in the radical sense of having no relationships through which he can even gain a reflection of his own self-understanding. His claims and those of his accusers are equally reasonable and absurd. We cannot be sure which is the case. Neither his own reasoning nor the disclosures from outside himself grant any secure knowledge of identity. He contains within himself both self-affirmations and self-destructive mechanisms, and both at the same time. The world outside him would appear to grant him a kind of existence if he would admit his guilt before absent accusers, but he is never even given the chance to formalize this kind of compromise. He is plunged into existence. What he thinks he remembers of a meaningful past is consistently contradicted by the disclosures from police and university colleagues. In the face of an apparently absurd world, he opts to enact his guilt, thus becoming guilty existentially. This final gesture of guilt-acceptance grants a kind of tragic stature to Taranne. We are left with an image of isolated man whose only means of asserting his identity is a gesture, and in this case a gesture by which he intensifies his isolation and guilt.

Adamov's man is alone, bewildered by the circumstances of his existence, bound by a sense of responsibility, though incapable of effectively discharging it, unable to achieve significance through language, and finally reduced to a gesture of alienation and withdrawal as the sole means of asserting identity. Both Pierre and Professor Taranne feel a responsibility toward their vocations: deciphering the manuscript in the case of Pierre, and university lecturing in the case of

Taranne. In differing ways, they both come to the realization
that language fails them. Their final gestures are made in silence and are gestures of self-alienation from their worlds. It
is true that Pierre is not faced with charges of guilt as is Taranne, but Pierre's inner sense of inadequacy before his task,
and the urgency he feels about some kind of resolution, are
equivalent to Taranne's being confronted with guilt from
outside himself and his sense of urgency for resolution of his
situation. In both cases, their essential isolation from the human community is further intensified and legitimized by their
final gestures.

In Adamov's vision, man is affirmed as a creature who has
responsibility, who is guilty in the face of failure to discharge
his responsibility, but who is caught in a metaphysical situation in which neither language nor reason can save him. All
efforts come to the same end: radical isolation and death.
Man's final act is a gesture of resignation. But this is a theatrical gesture, enacted in an event of the theatre and on a
stage taken by Adamov as a space to be filled. Thus man's
gesture of resignation takes on both the qualities of an artistic
resolution to his envisioned condition, as well as the symbolic
values of a metaphysical assertion. Without the theatrical
gesture there is no metaphysical assertion. We are not free to
abstract from the theatrical context a rational or linguistic
statement about man's fated situation. But held in tension
with the theatrical (the artistic) vision, the metaphysical assertion takes on its appropriate metaphorical form. The assertion is a matter of vision, not of reason, and in this sense is
a revelation. In Adamov's vision, man is revealed as both responsible and guilty, as isolated from his world and finally
reduced to a gesture which intensifies his exile.

AVANT-GARDE IMAGES OF MAN
IN A CHRISTIAN PERSPECTIVE

If the foregoing analyses of representative avant-garde playwrights and plays carry significance for Protestant theology, it is because the concern with man and his situation exemplified in this theatre brings pressure upon theology and its involvement with Christian anthropology. In anticipation of coming to some sort of terms with this pressure, the first two chapters of this study were devoted to a groundwork within theology and within the avant-garde theatre which would open discussion between the two.

The parallels and affinities between theology and theatrical criticism are evident. But so are the temptations to make theatrical criticism a crypto-theology. This temptation must be avoided at the same time that we assert a genuinely creative function for the playwright and genuine possibilities for revelation of man's metaphysical and spiritual situation in the theatrical event. From a theological perspective, God is as able to use theatre as he is any other event in history. But God and the playwright are not equals, and theology and theatrical criticism are not the same discourse. The Protestant principle allows us to discuss both theatre and theology in parallel terms, and, insofar as they both point beyond themselves to the depths of the human situation, they both attest to the void out of which new meaning and understanding of that human situation can come. What is assumed here?

Contained within the self-critical equipment of Protestantism is what Professor Paul Tillich calls the "Protestant principle." "What makes Protestantism Protestant is the fact that it transcends its own religious and confessional character, that it cannot be identified wholly with any of its particular historical forms."[1] The essence of this principle is that it protests any absolute claim made on behalf of any relative reality. Behind this principle lies the prophetic tradition of biblical faith which questions any religious or cultic form which becomes idolatrous in its claims for absolute necessity as the way of salvation (e.g., the Mosaic law). But as Tillich understands the Protestant principle, it "is the judge of every religious and cultural reality, including the religion and culture which calls itself 'Protestant.' "[2] This principle is

> the theological expression of the true relation between the unconditional and the conditioned or, religiously speaking, between God and man. As such, it is concerned with what theology calls "faith," namely, the state of mind in which we are grasped by the power of something unconditional which manifests itself to us as the ground and judge of our existence. The power grasping us in the state of faith is not a being beside others, not even the highest; it is not an object among objects, not even the greatest; but it is a quality of all beings and objects, the quality of pointing beyond themselves and their finite existence to the infinite, inexhaustible, and unapproachable depth of their being and meaning.[3]

For Tillich it is through what he calls the "theonomous depths" of things that we are grasped by ultimate reality. He likes to express this situation by the phrase, "Religion is the substance of culture and culture the form of religion."[4] In line with what we have already discussed concerning the death of God and the problematic character of modern human existence, Tillich asserts that the prevailing symbol for the theonomous depths of modern culture is a vacuum or void. But seen in the light of a theonomous analysis

> the vacuum of disintegration can become a vacuum out of which creation is possible, a "sacred void," so to speak, which brings a quality of waiting, of "not yet," of a being broken from above, into all our cultural creativity.[5]

A theonomous analysis of culture, then, leads to the establishment of the Protestant principle as a critical assumption. The possibility of being grasped anew by God through fresh cultural forms, fresh ideas, fresh experiences makes the Protestant principle a critical point of reference above all cultural expressions, including religion and theology. Through this principle theology becomes open to what the artists have to say. In the final analysis, for theological criticism the Protestant principle will also judge the insights of the artists as well as those of the theologians; it cuts both ways.

We come now to the place where the theologian can no longer avoid taking a stand in relation to culture, and in the present case this means in relation to assertions about man and his situation in the images of man presented in the avant-garde French theatre. Such a stand invites criticism from the other side of the dialogue. But if conversation is to proceed, the theologian must finally push beyond the kind of sensitive listening and looking we have tried to achieve in our analyses of the plays. He must say wherein these images, from his point of view, support a Christian assessment of man and wherein they fall short.

In the avant-garde presentation man's situation begins and ends in a void. This is to say that man is seen in a situational environment which is opaque to meanings beyond those possible in the situation itself. This is not to say that no meanings are possible; it is rather to point man inward toward himself and his immediate existential situation for what meaning may be found. Insofar as this presentation does indeed point man toward the depths of his immediate situation, it does feed into and support a theological assessment of the human situation which speaks of the necessity of looking squarely into the void of modern sensibility in order to see there the radical possibility of a new creation, a new word, a new consciousness of man's dependence upon God for meaning and significance in existence.

We have seen that Beckett's man is faced with this void and with the necessity of waiting upon it for a disclosure of meaning. That disclosure does not come, but Beckett's vision does encompass a proximate meaning which renders the necessity of waiting endurable. This proximate meaning is borne through his insistence that man is inescapably bound into relationship with his fellowman. To be sure, that relationship is potent for evil and destruction just as it is for companionship and compassion. But the same assertion is made from a theological viewpoint which insists upon man's inherent relational character and recognizes the possibility that this and all other aspects of existence may become demonic. It is sin which breaks this relationship in its inherent goodness and renders it demonic. Sin also issues in man's separation from his fellowman.

For discussion purposes it is possible to assert that sin means a state of separation between man and God for which man is responsible. Man's condition is the radical need to overcome this separation. His situation in relation to himself and his world is a state of separation reflecting his ultimate state of separation. The avant-garde images become powerful images of man's sinful state where they document this situation.

The characteristic response of the avant-garde man to his existence is a cry of anguish. It is not always an articulated or verbal cry. It is most often a brokenness of language, a distorted and frustrated gesture, which reveals an inner pain in response to his state of separation. The surface amenities by which our inner anguish is disguised in bourgeois society are broken through in the avant-garde images to disclose the crippled and pained nature of our efforts toward communication and relationship. The masks are put aside and man in his broken and isolated state is shown forth. Such a vision is at one with the theological assertion that man's sinful state of separation generates real pain and anguish, both mental and physical. Man's dis-eased state is symptomatic of his ultimate condition.

Adamov is most articulate in his identification of the state of separation with modern man's unnamed condition. And guilt is most clearly a consequence of this state in Adamov's vision. But Ionesco is similarly disposed to indicate man's sense of guilt. In both playwrights, we discern a vision of man's inability to deal satisfactorily with what he feels are his responsibilities and his consequent sense of guilt. This is not a question of psychological guilt feelings. In the avant-garde view, man is guilty in his separation, and his anguish arises in relation to his guilt. The problem, of course, emerges when we ask after the source of this guilt. In relation to whom or what is man guilty? There is no answer to this question. But there is guilt, and there is separation from self and world. Theology attests to the same condition in man but counters with the assertion that man is guilty in his self-regarding acts which contribute to and perpetuate his state of separation.

A parallel to the theological concept of man's self-regarding acts is the disclosure in the avant-garde theatre of an image of man who contributes to his state of separation through acts of self-alienation. The most powerful image of this action is Adamov's Professor Taranne. But Genet's Blacks can be seen in a similar light, as can Ionesco's Professor, who becomes victimized by his own rational and verbal abilities. From a theological point of view, the consequences of sin are death. If there is any unambiguously clear consequence of man's state of separation in the avant-garde images, it is the consequence of death. To be sure, death in these images can be seen in other ways as well. Death functions as a radical sign of human contingency, and, theologically speaking, this is a welcome recognition of concrete human reality in the midst of a culture which tries to escape from the fact of death. The bitter irony, of course, inheres in recent cultural history which has witnessed such wholesale man-wrought death. The avant-garde images of death point us toward both the reality of death and the demonic search for it by a dis-eased society. But in either case, Artaud was right that the sky can still fall on us and any genuine engagement with life must come to terms with contingency and death.

In one sense, the avant-garde theatre's concern with language and the possibilities of verbal communication is only another reflection within modern culture of a deep restlessness regarding man's linguistic abilities. While their concern is by no means identical, poetry criticism, linguistic analytical philosophy, modern Protestant theology in some of its movements, and other dimensions of cultural activity are caught up in the problem of language. That the avant-garde theatre should reflect this general concern is not surprising, but that language should be so radically dealt with is important. Particularly in Beckett's theatre we have seen how linguistic activity is one of the primary means by which his man comes to some kind of terms with the necessity of waiting, on the one hand, and with the problem of loneliness, on the other hand. Beckett's characters remark how their language games give them a sense of existing. This may be a rather slim affirmation of the relationship between language and existence, but it is an important affirmation when man is seen as dependent almost entirely upon his own inherent abilities for whatever significance and meaning is possible in his existence. This kind of affirmation supports a theological assessment of man which sees speaking as one of the fundamental ways in which dignity and significance are appropriately man's due.

It would be overstating the case to try to link Beckett's use of language to the theological tradition which has fastened upon the metaphor of speaking to delineate God's primary means of self-disclosure. This is not the only dimension of God's relationship to man in the Judeo-Christian tradition, but it is a basic one. And just because the metaphor of speech is so important to the theological tradition, the whole problem of speech as reflected in the avant-garde theatre takes on added meaning. We will see below some of the negative consequences of the avant-garde images in relation to language.

In Ionesco's theatre, primarily, and to some extent in Beckett's, the element of laughter takes on genuine significance. This is perhaps a minor but not less important dimension of the avant-garde images of man. When we laugh at the Bergsonian mechanisms, the puns, the logical absurdities, the gestural anticlimaxes of Ionesco's characters, we are made lucidly aware of the genuinely laughable dimension of human existence. It is not simply a question of a certain sense of humor saving us from complete abjection; it is rather that part of a serious engagement with the ambiguities and complexities of human existence must reveal the comic as well as the tragic dimensions of life. In both Ionesco and Beckett the tragic and comic are fused in such a way that these terms, in their traditional definitions, do not readily apply to the vision projected. But we laugh, nevertheless, and we laugh because part of man's greatness, to paraphrase Pascal, is to be aware that he is a comic being in the midst of cosmic ambiguity. It is very important for theology to be reminded that man has a comic dimension to his spirit, that he is capable both of laughable acts and of responses in laughter to the comic. Man's wholeness, whatever else it may mean, must certainly include this dimension. However, we are not dealing in the avant-garde images with a pure comic. The comic dimension is never far from the ironic and even the tragic. What we have

is often the kind of laughter described by one of the characters of the Belgian playwright, Michael de Ghelderode. The
King in *Escurial* tells his fool that he likes the kind of laughter
that has teeth in it.[6] This is often the laughter of the avant-
garde man, but its lucidity, irony, sometimes grating despair,
do not remove it from its place as an important dimension of
a vision of man.

Genet's theatre is of particular importance for its insistence
upon ritual as a means of coming to terms with existence.
What is involved here is the ritual action which catches up
man in his corporate relationships and relates him as a corporate being to those forces, emotions, experiences, hopes,
fears, and aspirations which constitute the groundwork of his
existence. Through the ritual act, man places himself in some
kind of continuing relationship with that prior community of
men through whom (in history and in thought) a tradition
of meaning and significance is mediated to the present generation. By means of ritualistically recounting the great events
of the past of a people or community and by enacting the
visions and prophesies of the heroes of the tradition, the present generation, both as initiates and as communicants, is given
direction and meaning for its life. Genet has once again
brought the theatre into relation with this ancient religious-
theatrical dimension of human spirit and activity. We may indeed quarrel with the meanings Genet evokes through his
use of ritual and with the evident failure of his ritual to place
his characters in relationship to a life-affirming realm of value,
but that his theatre points toward the ineluctable resources
of ritual for moving human sensibility to deeper levels of
awareness than those granted by superficial and habitual action is not to be gainsaid. And, certainly, part of the awareness
gained through ritual is that man stands in relation to a transcendent dimension of existence. For Genet this dimension is
the meaning centering in names, such as "Maids" and "Blacks,"
a dimension which transcends human existence but which

does not foster that existence. The ritual movement in Genet's theatre is from life to death, from human significance to nominalistic abstraction, but these are not the only alternatives for ritual action. His obvious trading upon the tradition of the Mass only points up by inversion the significance of ritual to the placement of man into relation with a life-affirming transcendence. While the liturgical tradition of Christianity may not function in this way for many contemporary men, it does not follow that all ritual must evoke death. Genet's achievement, from a theological point of view, is to remind us that men need ritual and that ritual can be powerful for life, if also for death.

Adamov's emphasis upon gesture is, perhaps, a kind of footnote to Genet's extensive employment of ritual. For Adamov, the individual—isolated, fearful, confused, guiltily separated man—employs gesture to disclose his situation. That the gestures possible for Adamov's man are either privately mystical or merely self-alienating should not obscure the reminder that words alone are not sufficient to encompass human meaning. By our gestures, also, we are known and come to know ourselves. Language can be seen from the viewpoint of linguistic gesture, and it is not mere sophistry to turn this around and see gesture as a language of communication between self and world. The outcome of gesturing in Adamov's vision is controlled by his perception of man in radical isolation, but we need to note the power of the gesture to express and underscore the vision, as well as to communicate it. A Protestant tradition which has tended to emphasize language to the exclusion of ritual and gesture can well afford to learn again of the gestural dimension of human action which points beyond itself in powerful ways to those depths of perception and meaning which language also symbolizes but does not totally encompass. One is reminded of the gesture of John the Baptist's pointing finger in Grünewald's famous Isenheim altarpiece crucifixion painting.

Perhaps enough comment has already been given to the question of communion in the avant-garde theatre. Without wishing to suggest any strict analogies, it is possible to assert that what takes place in the avant-garde theatre reflects the Apostle Paul's words when he says that by eating the bread and drinking the cup the Christian faithful show forth their Lord's death until he comes again. In many ways, what takes place in this theatre is a showing forth of man's death, and the void into which he goes, until a new man is born. This theatre lives in the Good Friday time. That a specific Christian affirmation of the Easter time is not possible for the avant-garde playwrights is not so important as their powerful reminder that it is only through Good Friday that Easter can come. If modern man is caught in the terrors and confusions, the betrayals and alienations of the Good Friday time, then he needs to reckon with his situation. It has certainly never been the Christian affirmation that man, by his own wits and energies, is capable of lifting himself out of his death-bound predicament. Neither is it the affirmation of the avant-garde playwrights. If their vision went no further than this, it would, nevertheless, be a needed reminder for theology and the Christian tradition that man stands in a situation of radical peril from which he cannot save himself. But perhaps, just perhaps, by facing his situation with all the honesty of which he is capable he may become open to a new vision, a new being granted from out of the depths. It is this possibility which enables theology, under the pressure of the Protestant principle, to embrace the avant-garde vision as a challenge to its own easy conformities to the bourgeois culture in which it is embedded in our time.

Many of the elements of the avant-garde images of man which are seen as supporting a Christian theological assessment of man can also be taken as inimical to this view. The Christian image of man as servant assumes that man, even in his sinfulness, has the potentiality for service. Given the one thing needful, faithful obedience to the image of the servant, man is enabled to become himself through the expression of those sensitivities and feelings which constitute his self-giving potentialities. In the Christian view, man as creature has an identity in relationship to God and to fellowman, he has a world which he shares in creaturehood, he has freedom and responsibility, he stands within history, and he participates in a realm of transcendent meaning mediated to him through his religious tradition. A Christian image of man needs to some-how encompass, or imply, at least these elements.

We have seen how difficult it is (if not indeed impossible) for man in the avant-garde images to achieve identity. Under the sign of the death of God, any relationship to deity is cut off for man. Only in Beckett's vision is there the possibility for the kind of qualitative human relationships which grant some sense of identity. But even his characters do not realize this possibility. Theologically understood, this kind of iden-tity is a faith-assertion which must be tested in the crucible of concrete human society. By whatever genesis, and more un-conscious than conscious, Beckett's tramps do sense the sig-nificance of compassionate relationships, though this sense is somewhat undercut by their doubt as to whether their ex-perience is real or in a dream. None of the characters in the other plays comes even close to achieving a demonstrable identity. When cut off from both God and any meaningful human tradition and community, man does not have an iden-tity. Individualistic efforts to achieve it end in Adamov's vision of the self-alienating gesture of withdrawal from what shreds of community may be possible.

In a Christian view, man is certainly subject to contin-gency, but he is not a pawn of forces outside himself, nor is he a victim of himself and his world. In the avant-garde images, man is seen primarily as one or another kind of victim. This is particularly true in Ionesco's plays. We have noted how Ionesco's vision sees man becoming victimized by language, by reason, by a world oppressed by its material nature, and by the relationships he does try to establish in his world.

In the previous section, we discussed the positive dimension to the avant-garde emphasis on language. Its negative side is revealed in the way in which language becomes an instrument of tyranny. This is more than a warning about propaganda in modern society, important as this warning is. This kind of assessment of man's linguistic ability quite undercuts the whole philosophical and theological emphasis upon the peculiar and precious nature of human language among the attributes of creation. We must not underestimate the ambiguity here, however. The avant-garde playwrights do use language to communicate to us the potential threat to spiritual life which language poses. The stance of a theological criticism at this point is perhaps best taken in a similarly ambiguous way. A Christian view of man affirms man's linguistic powers, and insofar as the avant-garde vision makes the same affirmation by implication, it is to be gratefully received. Insofar as the avant-garde vision simply presents man as a victim of language, the theological critic must demur.

The philosophical implications of the downgrading which reason receives in the avant-garde images are too various and far-reaching to be followed here. Suffice it to note that both in the biblical tradition and in the Christian theological tradition, a fairly high assessment has been given man's powers of reason. This is not the same thing as asserting that reason may save man from his condition. But it is to say that reason may aid man in assessing his situation and in manipulating those elements of his spiritual and physical situation which are permeable to reasoned action. A Christian view of man suggests that there certainly are limits to man's reason, but the precise definition of such limits is open to question. The "logic" that leads to Lucky's catastrophe of rational discourse in *Waiting for Godot* and to the dictim that "mathematics leads to philology, and philology leads to crime" in *The Lesson*, would appear to set limits to reason which are so close to the existing center of man as to render reason itself almost nonexistent. The avant-garde vision, at best, radically distrusts reason. What reach beyond his existent situation is possible for man is not a reach of reason, whatever else it might be in the way of gesture and language. It would appear that when man attempts to reason, he becomes a victim of his own ability and what facts he may garner concerning his situation do not add up to any rationally demonstrable meaning.

Avant-garde man simply does not have a world to which he is related as fellow creature. A Christian view of man insists that man does have a world through which God's gracious purposes are mediated, not exclusively, but certainly really. In a sense, a theological view insists that man has a metaphysical environment because he has a physical environment and that the two cannot be separated. This kind of view is reflected in Artaud's theories of *mise en scène* and metaphysics, but his intention is to manipulate the physical aspects of the theatrical event to reveal man's metaphysical situation. We have seen how Adamov comes closest to following Artaud at this point, though Beckett's miserable tree reflects something of the same vision. But this is a different thing from claiming all of creation as "the theatre of God's action." It is at this point that Nathan A. Scott, Jr.'s remark that the Christian critic must help the poet accept the world[7] becomes relevant. The avant-garde images escape the world of finitude despite, if not in consequence of, their intention to present a view of finite man. It is here, in an important way, that these images are different from those Scott cites. We are not dealing with angelism nor pure poetry nor even the "inebriation of Angst." But we are dealing with images which see man cut off from his world, or entirely engulfed by its material character.

Without a language which genuinely communicates, without reason, without a world, and without God, avant-garde man is radically thrown back upon himself and his relationships. It is evident, however, that little can be expected from his relationships to his fellowman if he has no real means of establishing them. A few gestures, a bit of ritual—these are his only means. In consequence, man becomes victimized by even what little he can muster in the way of outreach and empathy. All man-woman relationships are seriously questioned in these images. Marriage is more often a destructive state than anything approaching a relationship through which we become human. Friend and friend is a problematic possibility which is as potent for the Pozzo-Lucky vision as it is for the Vladimir-Estragon or Village-Virtue vision. A Christian view does not assert that easy and superficial relationships constitute genuine qualitative relationships which give substance and meaning to personal identity, but such a view does insist that man cannot escape his relational character and that all efforts at radical individualism are bound to fail. Again, we are faced with some ambiguity. The avant-garde images can be taken as powerful symbols of what can and does happen to men who do not live by faith. But this would be pressing the playwrights into a mold they do not readily espouse. Our job as Christian critics would be easier and more affirmative of the avant-garde if Ionesco had not insisted that "mockery, anguish, confusion, fear" constitute "essential" humanity. That such debilities are dimensions of man's existence is not to be denied. However, if we must speak of essences (a philosophical term and not a biblical-Christian term), we must fault the avant-garde images at this point. The radical isolation of avant-garde man, coupled with his victimization by his relationships, runs counter to a theological assessment of man which sees humanity in relational terms and under the pressure of the image of the servant.

We have seen the difficulty of the avant-garde images in affirming anything which might be called human freedom. We have seen some evidence of a sense of responsibility, primarily in relation to a search for personal identity, but we have not seen the kind of freedom which makes responsibility a genuine possibility. From a theological viewpoint there is neither human freedom without responsibility, nor is there possible a meaningful responsibility apart from its grounding in freedom of the will which directs action. This is a crucial issue in a theological image of man which sees anxiety and the temptation to self-regarding action precisely at the point where man experiences freedom, either to affirm his relatedness to God and the world or to seek to escape this relatedness through some form of self-alienating activity.[8] From this perspective it is not surprising the avant-garde images cannot make good on either man's sense of responsibility or on his self-identity.

In relation to the question of identity the issue of history also emerges. In a Christian view of man, it is only as the individual affirms for himself a stand within a living tradition of meaning and value, which has been held as the central commitment of an historical community of men, that he comes to a genuine sense of identity. The avant-garde images do not relate man to any such tradition. These images view man solely in a situational relationship to existence. This situation does not participate in an historical continuum which both carries and is supported by deep affirmations of man's relationship to his world and to God. This judgment does not deny the dramatic intensity and existential thrust made possible by the avant-garde limitation to situation vision. It is precisely this compression, almost into the existentialist "moment," that pushes the theatrical vision into the depths of the void. But these are not the only spatial metaphors which point toward the sources of meaning in existence. The horizontal dimension of historical tradition is also significant for human identity. This dimension of man's relatedness to the human past is lacking in the avant-garde images.

Without history beyond the situation, without the other elements noted above, it is problematic indeed to locate within the avant-garde images of man where transcendence might be found. So far as the images themselves are concerned, we must say that transcendence, that is, meaning from beyond the situation, is not envisioned in the avant-garde view of life. But we have seen throughout the preceding chapters of analysis how important it is to remember that we are dealing with theatrical images. This fact has two directions of referential significance. One is that just implied: the images in their poetic significance. The other is that theatre is a communal activity which catches up playwright, actors, and audience into one public event of spirit, mind, and body. In this sense, the images certainly do look outward in self-transcending fashion, both to the "circumambient world" of which they are a part and to the beliefs of the playwright who has projected them into their theatrical form. This kind of transcendence is not the same thing as asserting the need for divine transcendence as a constitutive element of a world view and of a vision of man. But it does allow us to move beyond the images as poetic statements and consider the kind of issues discussed above. It also enables us to ask the playwrights where their desire to communicate a vision of man finds its ultimate sanctions and values. From a theological perspective the playwrights need to bring, if they have not already done so, to the level of self-conscious awareness the assumptions about man as a being of worth which prompt them to cry out in warning for him. They may indeed not be able or willing to relate their concern for man to anything approaching a traditionally understood concept of God. But the theological critic will insist that God is, nevertheless, there, both in the creative act of vision and as ultimate end in which all life-affirming transcendence is grounded.

Some implications for the continuing apologetic task of theology in relation to culture have been evident, if not explicit, throughout the foregoing discussions. The conclusion to this study will simply underscore some of these by suggesting future agenda for theology.

It is of particular importance that theology be aware of the power of the avant-garde images for evoking a radical sense of human contingency. It is by no means clear that recent events of war and destruction have been sufficient to convince modern men of the terrible struggle which must be waged against death in the name of life. There is a curious and perverse manner in which, at least in America, our disinclination to take personal death seriously (as evidenced in our ghastly commercial burial practices) seems to aid a vast movement in the culture toward nihilism and mass suicide. A theology which insists that individual death is significant, and which affirms life and the power of God to overcome death, needs to take seriously those images which most powerfully evoke the seriousness and inescapability of personal death, but in so doing to affirm the precious and precarious value of life. This the avant-garde images of man, in many ways, achieve. How this cultural data can best be appropriated for theology's task of rendering understandable and clear the claims of the Christian gospel on our lives is, of course, open to far greater questioning and discussion than is provided in this study.

Further, it is of particular importance that theology appreciate the focus upon concrete particularity in the avant-garde images of man. There is a peculiarly persuasive quality about the situational emphasis of these images which recommends to our theologizing the need to pay attention to the particularities of human experience. We need to take men in their concrete existential situations and discover there the means of communicating the gospel. The avant-garde images help us to focus on this kind of concreteness. They evoke the loneliness and isolation of particular individuals. It is the death of particular men, regardless of the generic and typological manner in which many of the avant-garde characters are presented, which must be given attention. Precisely because identity is so fundamentally difficult to achieve for the avant-garde man, theology must address this man in his isolation, fear, confusion, and expectation of death.

There has gone on within the boundaries of modern theology considerable debate as to the relative merits of dogmatic and philosophical bases for the theological task. Perhaps a recapturing of some of the qualities, both apologetic and systematic, of the ancient allegorical methods of dealing with the data of culture as useful to the theological task can be achieved if we become open to something of the imaginative vision of man and his situation demonstrated in the avant-garde playwrights. This is not an appeal for the return of strict allegorical distortion of the culture to meet theological assumptions. It is, rather, the suggestion that much of the imaginative vision evident in the biblical materials should suggest to us that God uses the imagination as well as reason and events to disclose himself and his purposes to us. We must test the spirits, but we must become open to them before we can legitimately test them. This study has attempted to do just this. More needs to be done.

A final note is that theology must recognize that many institutions besides the church carry genuine life and renewal through their structures. This is certainly true of the theatre. The theatre as institution is not a church, but the parallels between the theatre event and public worship in the church are so evident as to open the way for much fruitful inter-change of vision and experience between churchmen and men of the theatre. This is not to suggest that the theatre needs to be imported into the church. We have already had too much of the business of controlling the lights, getting in some dance, using so-called chancel drama as a gimmick to somehow convince otherwise ignorant churchgoers that they can be both entertained and instructed in the mysteries of the faith. No, not this. But across the boundaries of church and theatre as living institutions, mutual recognition that both similarities and differences of function need to be kept clear, and that in making these clear, each will be strengthened in its proper approach to the human spirit for nurture and inspiriting— this is what needs to be achieved. The church cannot well ab-dicate its covenant to be God's people in the world and to celebrate this relationship through public worship. Nor can the theatre deny to itself its own proper power as an energizer and exalter of the human spirit.

> The theatrical profession may protest as much as it likes, the theologians may protest, and the majority of those who see our plays would probably be amazed to hear it, but the the-atre is a religious institution devoted entirely to the exaltation of the spirit of man. It is an attempt to justify, not the ways of God to man, but the ways of man to himself. It is an attempt to prove that man has a dignity and a destiny, that his life is worth living, that he is not purely animal and without pur-pose. There is no doubt in my mind that our theatre, instead of being, as the evangelical ministers used to believe, the gate-way to hell, is as much of a worship as the theatre of the Greeks, and has exactly the same meaning in our lives.[9]

The theologian and the layman need to hear this claim and place it over against their own experience as members of a worshipping community of those who believe that God's own purposes are concretely fulfilled, at least in partial ways, through the visions and creations of the human spirit.

NOTES

PREFACE

1. Cf. Paul Tillich, *The Protestant Era,* trans. James Luther Adams (Chicago: The University of Chicago Press, 1948), *passim.*
2. Gerardus van der Leeuw, *Sacred and Profane Beauty,* trans. David E. Green (New York: Holt, Rinehart and Winston 1963), p. 3.
3. *Ibid.,* p. 4.
4. Nathan A. Scott, Jr., *Modern Literature and the Religious Frontier* (New York: Harper & Brothers, 1958), p. 5.
5. *Ibid.,* p. 16.
6. Allen Tate, *On the Limits of Poetry* (New York: Swallow Press and W. Morrow and Co., 1948), p. 4.
7. Paul Tillich, *Systematic Theology* (Chicago: The University of Chicago Press, 1951), Vol. I, pp. 8 ff.
8. Scott, *op. cit.,* pp. 129-134. This is a useful bibliography.
9. Cf. T. S. Eliot, *After Strange Gods: A Primer of Modern Heresy* (New York: Harcourt, Brace and Co., 1934), and Amos N. Wilder, *The Spiritual Aspects of the New Poetry* (New York, London: Harper & Brothers, Publishers, 1940). Wilder's book was especially formative for the movement of theological criticism of literature.

CHAPTER 1

1. Gabriel Vahanian, *The Death of God* (New York: George Braziller, 1961), p. 168.
2. The term "mytho-poetic" is intended to suggest the inescapably symbolic nature of religious language. That such is the case with religious language is attested to by thinkers within as well as outside the Christian tradition. Cf. works on language by R. Bultmann, E. Cassirer, S. K. Langer, P. Tillich, W. M. Urban, and A. N. Wilder.
3. Indeed the notion of relationship is definitive for the meaning of religion in the Bible. Religion, in biblical understanding, is not

first of all a matter of cult, but rather religion is that sphere of experience in which relationships of love, judgment, and forgiveness are constitutive of man's place in the world vis-à-vis both God and fellowman. This understanding is articulated in the twofold commandment regarding love of God and love of neighbor.

4. Throughout the New Testament, and particularly in Johannine thought, eternal life in God's kingdom is both a present reality and a future event in which what has begun to take place through Christ will be fulfilled. This emphasis brings particular pressure upon the quality of present human relationships and relates man to God's *telos* by way of the concrete particularity of his day-to-day existence. Cf. Amos N. Wilder, *New Testament Faith for Today* (New York: Harper & Brothers, Publishers, 1955), pp. 148 ff.

5. Van der Leeuw, *op. cit.*, pp. 304 ff.

6. *Ibid.*, p. 310.

7. *Ibid.*, p. 312.

8. John Calvin, *Institutes of the Christian Religion*, trans. Henry Beveridge (London: James Clarke and Co., 1953), Vol. I, p. 164.

9. Van der Leeuw, *op. cit.*, p. 315.

10. *Ibid.*, pp. 322 f.

11. *Ibid.*, p. 327.

12. Quoted in Roland M. Frye, *Perspective on Man: Literature and the Christian Tradition* (Philadelphia: The Westminster Press, 1961), p. 59.

13. Quoted in *ibid.*, p. 80.

14. *Ibid.*, pp. 13 f.

15. Quoted in *ibid.*, p. 13.

16. Calvin, *op. cit.*, p. 236.

17. Quoted in Frye, *op. cit.*, p. 94.

18. Quoted in *ibid.*, p. 121.

19. Irving Babbitt, *On Being Creative and Other Essays* (Boston and New York: Houghton Mifflin Company, 1932), p. 5.

20. Scott, *op. cit.*, p. 28.

21. Quoted in *ibid.*, p. 22.

22. *Ibid.*, p. 25

23. Quoted in *ibid.*, p. 27.

24. Stanley Romain Hopper, ed., *Spiritual Problems in Contemporary Literature* (New York: Harper & Brothers, Publishers, 1957, Harper Torchbooks), p. 176.

25. Jacques Maritain, *Creative Intuition in Art and Poetry* (New York: Pantheon Books, 1953), p. 115.

26. *Ibid.*, p. 126.

27. Scott, *op. cit.*, p. 32.

28. Frye, *op. cit.*, p. 15.

29. William F. Lynch, S. J., *Christ and Apollo* (New York: Sheed and Ward, 1960), p. 7.

30. Vahanian, *op. cit.*, pp. 96 f.

31. Scott, *op. cit.*, p. 61.

32. Cf. particularly Erich Auerbach, *Mimesis*, trans. Willard R. Trask (Princeton: Princeton University Press, 1953).

33. Amos N. Wilder, *Otherworldliness and the New Testament* (New York: Harper & Brothers, Publishers, 1954), pp. 36. f.

34. *Ibid.*, pp. 30 f.

CHAPTER 2

1. For a survey of religious drama in the contemporary French theatre see Martin Esslin, *The Theatre of the Absurd* (Garden City: Doubleday and Company, 1961, Anchor Books), pp. 312 ff.; Wallace Fowlie, *Dionysus in Paris* (New York: Meridian Books, 1960), pp. 18 ff.; Jacques Guicharnaud and June Beckelman, *Modern French Theatre from Giraudoux to Beckett* (New Haven: Yale University Press, 1961), pp. 69 ff.

2. Friedrich W. Nietzsche, *The Portable Nietzsche*, trans. Walter Kaufmann (New York: The Viking Press, 1954), pp. 103 ff.

3. Quoted in Finley Eversole, ed., *Christian Faith and the Contemporary Arts* (New York-Nashville: Abingdon Press, 1962), p. 50.

4. Rainer Maria Rilke, *Letters of Rainer Maria Rilke*, trans. Jane Bannard Greene and M. D. Herter Norton (New York: W. W. Norton and Co., 1947), Vol. II, p. 324.

5. Quoted in Vahanian, *op. cit.*, p. 122.

6. Esslin, *op. cit.*, p. 291.

7. Arthur Adamov, "The Endless Humiliation," trans. Richard Howard, *Evergreen Review*, Vol. 2, No. 8 (Spring, 1959), pp. 66 f.

8. Cf. Richard E. Sherrell, "The Case Against God in Contemporary French Drama," *Religion in Life*, Vol. XXXI, No. 4 (Autumn, 1962).

9. Cf. Wallace Fowlie, *Age of Surrealism* (Bloomington: Indiana University Press, 1960), pp. 24 ff.

10. Quoted in Robert W. Corrigan (ed.), *The New Theatre of Europe*, Vol. 1 (New York: Dell Publishing Co., Inc., 1962, A Delta Book), p. 13.

11. Artaud tried to incorporate his ideas in a Renaissance play, *Les Cinci*. However, the production of *Les Cinci* in 1935 was a failure. Cf. Leonard Cabell Pronko, *Avant-Garde: The Experimental Theater in France* (Berkeley: University of California Press, 1962), p. 16.

12. Antonin Artaud, *The Theatre and Its Double,* trans. Mary Caroline Richards (New York: Grove Press, Inc., 1958), p. 79.

13. *Ibid.,* p. 37.

14. *Ibid.*

15. *Ibid.,* p. 39.

16. *Ibid.,* p. 41.

17. *Ibid.,* p. 44.

18. *Ibid.,* p. 46.

19. *Ibid.,* p. 13.

20. Guicharnaud, *op. cit.,* p. 230.

21. Esslin, *op. cit.,* p. 293.

22. *Ibid.,* pp. 229 ff.

23. Jacques Maritain and Jean Cocteau, *Art and Faith* (New York: Philosophical Library, 1948), p. 87.

24. *Ibid.,* pp. 54 f.

CHAPTER 3

1. Samuel Beckett, *Waiting for Godot,* trans. the author (New York: Grove Press, Inc., 1954), p. 7, copyright © 1954 by Grove Press. All further references to this play will be noted simply by the page numbers.

2. Cf. Edith G. Kern, "Drama Stripped for Inaction: Beckett's *Godot,*" *Yale French Studies,* Vol. 14.

3. Charles S. McCoy, "*Waiting for Godot*: A Biblical Appraisal," *Religion in Life,* Vol. XXVIII, No. 4 (Autumn, 1959).

4. Jean-Jacques Mayoux, "The Theatre of Samuel Beckett," *Perspective,* Vol. II, No. 3 (Autumn, 1959), p. 145.

5. Quoted in Esslin, *op. cit.,* pp. 19 f.

6. Cited in *ibid.,* p. 43.

7. Quoted in *ibid.,* p. 44.

8. Cf. Robert Champigny, "Interprétation de *En Attendant Godot,*" *PMLA,* Vol. LXXV, No. 3 (June, 1960). Champigny defers to the similarity between Beckett's language games and the concept of language games as developed by Ludwig Wittgenstein.

9. Kenneth Rexroth, "The Point Is Irrelevance," *The Nation,* Vol. 182 (April 14, 1956), p. 328.

CHAPTER 4

1. A fuller discussion of these matters is to be found in Esslin, *op. cit.,* and Leonard C. Pronko, *op. cit.*

2. Eugène Ionesco, "The Point of Departure," trans. Leonard C. Pronko, *Theatre Arts,* Vol. XLII, No. 6 (June, 1958), p. 18.

3. *Ibid.,* p. 3.

4. *Ibid.*, p. 17.

5. *Ibid.*

6. *Ibid.*, p. 18.

7. Eugène Ionesco, "Discovering the Theatre," trans. Leonard C. Pronko, *Tulane Drama Review*, Vol. 4, No. 1 (September, 1959), p. 6.

8. Eugène Ionesco, "The World of Ionesco," *Tulane Drama Review*, Vol. 3, No. 1 (October, 1958), p. 48.

9. Eugène Ionesco, "Notes on My Theatre," trans. Leonard C. Pronko, *Tulane Drama Review*, Vol. 7, No. 3 (Spring, 1963), p. 132.

10. *Ibid.*, p. 128.

11. *Ibid.*, p. 159.

12. Eugène Ionesco, *Four Plays*, trans. Donald M. Allen (New York: Grove Press, Inc., 1958), copyright © 1958 by Grove Press, Inc., pp. 43 ff. All further references to the text of *The Lesson* will be noted simply by the page numbers.

13. *Ibid.*, pp. 7 f.

14. Eugène Ionesco, "The Tragedy of Language," trans. Jack Undank, *Tulane Drama Review*, Vol. 4, No. 3 (March, 1960), p. 13.

15. J. S. Doubrovsky, "Ionesco and the Comedy of Absurdity," *Yale French Studies*, No. 23 (Summer, 1959), p. 8.

16. Eugène Ionesco, *Three Plays*, trans. Donald Watson (New York: Grove Press, Inc., 1958), © John Calder (Publishers) Limited 1958, pp. 117-166. All further references to the text of *Victims of Duty* will be noted simply by the page numbers.

17. Pronko, *op. cit.*, p. 86.

18. Ionesco, *Four Plays*, pp. 111 ff.

19. Ionesco, *Three Plays*, pp. 3-89.

20. Cf. Doubrovsky, cited in Esslin, *op. cit.*, pp. 103 ff., for a third alternative.

21. Jean Vannier, "A Theatre of Language," trans. Leonard C. Pronko, *Tulane Drama Review*, Vol. 7, No. 3 (Spring, 1963), p. 181.

22. *Ibid.*, p. 186.

23. Eugène Ionesco, "Theatre and Anti-Theatre," trans. Leonard C. Pronko, *Theatre Arts*, Vol. XLII, No. 6 (June, 1958), p. 18.

24. Doubrovsky, *op. cit.*, p. 5.

25. Robert W. Corrigan, "The Theatre in Search of a Fix," *Tulane Drama Review*, Vol. 5, No. 4 (June, 1961), p. 21.

26. Ionesco, "The World of Ionesco," p. 46.

CHAPTER 5

1. Jean-Paul Sartre, *Saint Genet: Actor and Martyr*, trans. Bernard Frechtman (New York: George Braziller, 1963).

2. Jean Genet, "A Note on Theatre," trans. Bernard Frechtman, *Tulane Drama Review*, Vol. 7, No. 3 (Spring, 1963), p. 37.

3. *Ibid.*, p. 38.

4. *Ibid.*, pp. 39 f.

5. *Ibid.*, p. 40.

6. Oreste F. Pucciani, "Tragedy, Genet and *The Maids*," *Tulane Drama Review*, Vol. 7, No. 3 (Spring, 1963), pp. 44 f.

7. J. M. Svendson, "Corydon Revisited: A Reminder on Genet," *Tulane Drama Review*, Vol. 7, No. 3 (Spring, 1963), p. 103.

8. Jean Genet, *The Maids and Deathwatch*, trans. Bernard Frechtman (New York: Grove Press, Inc., 1954), copyright © 1954 by Bernard Frechtman. All further references to *The Maids* will be noted simply by the page numbers.

9. Sartre, *op. cit.*, p. 616.

10. *Ibid.*, pp. 73 ff.

11. *Ibid.*, p. 611.

12. Marc Pierret, "Genet's New Play: *The Screens*," trans. Rima Drell Reck, *Tulane Drama Review*, Vol. 7, No. 3 (Spring, 1963), p. 97.

13. Jean Genet, *The Blacks: A Clown Show*, trans. Bernard Frechtman (New York: Grove Press, Inc., 1960), copyright © 1960 by Bernard Frechtman. All further references to the text of *The Blacks* will be noted simply by the page numbers.

14. *Ibid.*

15. Cf. Jean Genet, "To a Would-Be Producer," trans. Bernard Frechtman, *Tulane Drama Review*, Vol. 7, No. 3 (Spring, 1963). In this note, Genet refuses permission for a Warsaw production of *The Blacks* because the producer wanted to use a white cast.

16. Esslin, *op. cit.*, p. 167.

17. Sartre, *op. cit.*, p. 2.

18. Esslin, *op. cit.*, p. 161.

19. Pucciani, *op. cit.*, p. 44.

20. Esslin, *op. cit.*, p. 141.

CHAPTER 6

1. Arthur Adamov, "Note Préliminaire," *Théâtre*, Vol. II (Paris: Gallimard, 1955), copyright by Librairie Gallimard, 1955, p. 8.

2. Arthur Adamov, *Théâtre*, Vol. I (Paris: Gallimard, 1953), copyright by Librairie Gallimard, 1953, pp. 7 ff.

3. Adamov, "Note Préliminaire," *op. cit.*, p. 8.

4. Cited in Esslin, *op. cit.*, p. 51.

5. Adamov, "The Endless Humiliation," *op. cit.*, p. 64.

6. *Ibid.*, p. 66.

7. *Ibid.,* p. 67.
8. *Ibid.*
9. *Ibid.*
10. *Ibid.,* p. 70.
11. *Ibid.,* pp. 70 f.
12. *Ibid.,* p. 76.
13. *Ibid.,* p. 66.
14. *Ibid.,* p. 67.
15. *Ibid.,* p. 95.
16. Adamov, "Note Préliminaire," *op. cit.,* p. 9.
17. Adamov, "The Endless Humiliation," *op. cit.,* p. 84.
18. *Ibid.,* p. 80.
19. Pronko, *op. cit.,* p. 131.
20. Esslin, *op. cit.,* p. 77.
21. Adamov, *Théâtre,* Vol. I, pp. 55 ff.
22. Pronko, *op. cit.,* p. 138.
23. Adamov, *Théâtre,* Vol. I, p. 86. This is the writer's unauthorized translation of the French text which reads: "Pourquoi dit-on: 'Il arrive?' Qui est ce 'il,' que veut-il de moi? Pourquoi dit-on 'par' terre, plutôt que 'a' ou 'sur'? J'ai perdu trop de temps à réfléchir sur ces choses. Ce qu'il me faut, ce n'est pas le sens des mots, c'est leur volume et leur corps mouvant. Je ne chercherai plus rien. J'attendrai dans le silence, immobile. Je deviendrai très attentif. Il faut que je parte le plus vite possible."
24. Adamov, *Théâtre,* Vol. I, pp. 143 ff.
25. Adamov, *Théâtre,* Vol. II, pp. 65 ff.
26. Esslin, *op. cit.,* p. 54.
27. Adamov, "Note Préliminaire," *op. cit.,* pp. 9 f.
28. Pronko, *op. cit.,* p. 139.
29. Arthur Adamov, "Professor Taranne," trans. Albert Bermel, found in *Four Modern French Comedies* (New York: G. P. Putnam's Sons, 1960, Capricorn Books), © 1960, G. P. Putnam's Sons, pp. 125 ff. All references to the text of *Professor Taranne* will be noted simply by the page numbers.
30. Cf. Adamov, "Note Préliminaire," *op. cit.,* p. 13.
31. *Ibid.,* p. 12.
32. *Ibid.,* p. 13.
33. Adamov, *Théâtre,* Vol. II, pp. 19 ff.
34. *Ibid.,* pp. 95 ff.

CHAPTER 7

1. Tillich, *The Protestant Era,* p. 162.
2. *Ibid.,* p. 163.

3. *Ibid.*

4. *Ibid.*, p. 57. Cf. also Paul Tillich, *Theology of Culture*, ed. Robert C. Kimball (New York: Oxford University Press, 1959), p. 42.

5. Tillich, *The Protestant Era*, p. 60.

6. Michael de Ghelderode, "Escurial," found in *The Modern Theatre*, Eric Bently, ed. (Garden City, N.Y.: Doubleday and Company, Inc., 1957, Doubleday Anchor Books), Vol. 5, p. 168.

7. Cf. Scott, *op. cit.*, pp. 61-64.

8. Cf. Reinhold Niebuhr, *The Nature and Destiny of Man*, Vol. I (New York: Charles Scribner's Sons, 1951), pp. 178 ff.

9. Maxwell Anderson, *Candle in the Wind* (Washington, D.C.: Anderson House, 1941), pp. x-xi.

BIBLIOGRAPHY

Adamov, Arthur. "Professor Taranne." Translated by Albert Bermel. *Four Modern French Comedies.* New York: B. P. Putnam's Sons. 1960.

——. *Théâtre.* Vol. I. Paris: Gallimard, 1953.

——. *Théâtre.* Vol. II. Paris: Gallimard, 1955.

——. "The Endless Humiliation," translated by Richard Howard, *Evergreen Review,* Vol. 2, No. 8 (Spring, 1959).

Anderson, Maxwell. *Candle in the Wind.* Washington, D.C.: Anderson House, 1941.

Artaud, Antonin. *The Theatre and Its Double.* Translated by Mary Caroline Richards. New York: Grove Press, Inc., 1958.

Auerbach, Erich. *Mimesis.* Translated by Willard Trask. Garden City, N.Y.: Doubleday & Company, Inc., 1957. Doubleday Anchor Books.

Babbitt, Irving. *On Being Creative and Other Essays.* Boston and New York: Houghton Mifflin Company, 1932.

Beckett, Samuel. *Waiting for Godot.* Translated by the author. New York: Grove Press, Inc., 1954.

Calvin, John. *Institutes of the Christian Religion.* Translated by Henry Beveridge. Vol. I. London: James Clarke and Co., 1953.

Champigny, Robert. "Interprétation de *En Attendant Godot,*" *PMLA,* Vol. LXXV, No. 3 (June, 1960).

Corrigan, Robert W. (ed.). *The New Theatre of Europe,* Vol. I. New York: Dell Publishing Company, Inc., 1962. A Delta Book.

——. "The Theatre in Search of a Fix," *Tulane Drama Review,* Vol. 5, No. 4 (June, 1961).

De Ghelderode, Michael. "Escurial," found in *The Modern Theatre,* Eric Bently (ed.). Garden City, N.Y.: Doubleday and Company, Inc., 1957. Doubleday Anchor Books, Vol. 5, p. 168.

Doubrovsky, J. S. "Ionesco and the Comedy of Absurdity," *Yale French Studies,* No. 23 (Summer, 1959).

Eliot, T. S. *After Strange Gods: A Primer of Modern Heresy.* New York: Harcourt, Brace and Company, 1934.

Esslin, Martin. *The Theatre of the Absurd.* Garden City, N.Y.: Doubleday and Company, 1961, Doubleday Anchor Books.

Eversole, Finley (ed.). *Christian Faith and the Contemporary Arts.* New York-Nashville: Abingdon Press, 1962.

Fowlie, Wallace. *Age of Surrealism.* Bloomington: Indiana University Press, 1960.

———. *Dionysus in Paris.* New York: Meridan Books, 1960.

Frye, Roland M. *Perspective on Man: Literature and the Christian Tradition.* Philadelphia: The Westminster Press, 1961.

Genet, Jean. "A Note on Theatre," translated by Bernard Frechtman, *Tulane Drama Review,* Vol. 7, No. 3 (Spring, 1963).

———. *The Blacks: A Clown Show.* Translated by Bernard Frechtman. New York: Grove Press, Inc., 1960.

———. *The Maids and Deathwatch.* Translated by Bernard Frechtman. New York: Grove Press, Inc., 1954.

———. "To a Would-Be Producer," translated by Bernard Frechtman, *Tulane Drama Review,* Vol. 7, No. 3 (Spring, 1963).

Guicharnaud, Jacques and Beckelman, June. *Modern French Theatre from Giraudoux to Beckett.* New Haven: Yale University Press, 1961.

Hopper, Stanley R. (ed.). *Spiritual Problems in Contemporary Literature.* New York: Harper & Brothers, Publishers, 1957. Harper Torchbooks.

Ionesco, Eugène. "Discovering the Theatre," translated by Leonard C. Pronko, *Tulane Drama Review,* Vol. 4, No. 1 (September, 1959).

———. *Four Plays.* Translated by Donald M. Allen. New York: Grove Press, 1958.

———. "Notes on My Theatre," translated by Leonard C. Pronko, *Tulane Drama Review,* Vol. 7, No. 3 (Spring, 1963).

———. "The Point of Departure," translated by Leonard C. Pronko, *Theatre Arts,* Vol. XLII, No. 6 (June, 1958).

———. "Theatre and Anti-Theatre," translated by Leonard C. Pronko, *Theatre Arts,* Vol. XLII, No. 6 (June, 1958).

———. "The Tragedy of Language," translated by Jack Undank, *Tulane Drama Review,* Vol. 4, No. 3 (March, 1960).

———. "The World of Ionesco," *Tulane Drama Review,* Vol. 3, No. 1 (October, 1958).

———. *Three Plays: Amédée, The New Testament, Victims of Duty.* Translated by Donald Watson. New York: Grove Press, Inc., 1958.

Kahler, Erich. *Man the Measure.* New York: Pantheon Books, Inc., 1943.

Kern, Edith. "Drama Stripped for Inaction: Beckett's *Godot,*" *Yale French Studies,* Vol. 14.

Bibliography

Lynch, William F., S. J. *Christ and Apollo*. New York: Sheed and Ward, 1960.
Maritain, Jacques and Cocteau, Jean. *Art and Faith*. New York: Philosophical Library, 1948.
Maritain, Jacques. *Creative Intuition in Art and Poetry*. New York: Pantheon Books, 1953.
Mayoux, Jean-Jacques. "The Theatre of Samuel Beckett," *Perspective*, Vol. 11, No. 3 (Autumn, 1959).
McCoy, Charles S. "*Waiting for Godot*: A Biblical Appraisal," *Religion in Life*, Vol. XXVIII, No. 4 (Autumn, 1959).
Niebuhr, Reinhold. *The Nature and Destiny of Man*. Vol. I. New York: Charles Scribner's Sons, 1941.
Niebuhr, Reinhold. *The Nature and Destiny of Man*. Vol. II. New York: Charles Scribner's Sons, 1943.
Nietzsche, Friedrich. *The Portable Nietzsche*. Translated by Walter Kaufmann. New York: The Viking Press, 1954.
Pierret, Marc. "Genet's New Play: *The Screens*," translated by Rima Drell Reck, *Tulane Drama Review*, Vol. 7, No. 3 (Spring, 1963).
Pronko, Leonard C. *Avant-Garde: The Experimental Theater in France*. Berkeley and Los Angeles: University of California Press, 1962.
Pucciani, Oreste F. "Tragedy, Genet and *The Maids*," *Tulane Drama Review*, Vol. 7, No. 3 (Spring, 1963).
Rexroth, Kenneth. "The Point Is Irrelevance," *The Nation*, Vol. 182 (April 14, 1956).
Rilke, Rainer Maria. *Letters of Rainer Maria Rilke*. Vol. II. Translated by Jane Bannard Greene and M. D. Herter Norton. New York: Norton and Company, Inc., 1947.
Sartre, Jean-Paul. *Saint Genet: Actor and Martyr*. Translated by Bernard Frechtman. New York: George Braziller, 1963.
Scott, Nathan A., Jr. *Modern Literature and the Religious Frontier*. New York: Harper & Brothers, 1958.
Sherrell, Richard E. "The Case Against God in Contemporary French Drama," *Religion in Life*, Vol. XXXI, No. 4 (Autumn, 1962).
Svendsen, J. M. "Corydon Revisited: A Reminder on Genet," *Tulane Drama Review*, Vol. 7, No. 3 (Spring, 1963).
Tate, Allen. *On the Limits of Poetry*. New York: Swallow Press and W. Morrow and Company, 1948.
Tillich, Paul. *Systematic Theology*, Vol. I. Chicago, Ill.: The University of Chicago Press, 1951.
———. *Systematic Theology*, Vol. II. Chicago, Ill.: The University of Chicago Press, 1957.

————. *The Protestant Era.* Translated by James Luther Adams. Chicago, Ill.: The University of Chicago Press, 1948.

————. *Theology of Culture.* Edited by Robert C. Kimball. New York: Oxford University Press, 1959.

Vahanian, Gabriel. *The Death of God.* New York: George Braziller, 1961.

Van der Leeuw, Gerardus. *Sacred and Profane Beauty: The Holy in Art.* Translated by David E. Green. New York: Holt, Rinehart and Winston, 1963.

Vannier, Jean. "A Theatre of Language," translated by Leonard C. Pronko, *Tulane Drama Review,* Vol. 7, No. 3 (Spring, 1963).

Wilder, Amos N. *New Testament Faith for Today.* New York: Harper & Brothers, 1955.

————. *Otherworldliness and the New Testament.* New York: Harper & Brothers, Publishers, 1954.

————. *The Spiritual Aspects of the New Poetry.* New York, London: Harper & Brothers, 1940.